NOTHING COMPARES TO YOU

What Sinéad O'Connor Means to Us

Edited by
SONYA HUBER and MARTHA BAYNE

ONE SIGNAL PUBLISHERS
ATRIA
NEW YORK AMSTERDAM/ANTWERP LONDON TORONTO SYDNEY/MELBOURNE NEW DELHI

ONE SIGNAL PUBLISHERS

ATRIA

An Imprint of Simon & Schuster, LLC
1230 Avenue of the Americas
New York, NY 10020

First One Signal Publishers/Atria Paperback edition August 2026

ONE SIGNAL PUBLISHERS / ATRIA PAPERBACK and colophon are registered trademarks of Simon & Schuster, LLC

Interior design by Esther Paradelo

Manufactured in the United States of America

1 3 5 7 9 10 8 6 4 2

Library of Congress Cataloging-in-Publication Data has been applied for.

ISBN 978-1-6680-7833-4
ISBN 978-1-6680-7834-1 (pbk)
ISBN 978-1-6680-7835-8 (ebook)

For all the singers and all the fighters

CONTENTS

Just as Sinéad O'Connor deployed her artistry to hold the darker material of human existence to the light, so, too, aims this book. Some of the essays collected here address difficult and often painful subjects, including child abuse, sexual assault, racialized violence, and suicide. O'Connor's candor about her own struggle to find supportive mental health care, and her fight to secure access to such care for all in need, that they might feel less alone, is a cornerstone of her lasting legacy. If you or a loved one are struggling with trauma or thoughts of self-harm, readers in the United States can access the 988 Suicide and Crisis Lifeline (https://988lifeline.org) by dialing 988 to be connected to a national network of mental health professionals and crisis centers. For peer support via a "warmline" staffed by others with personal experience living with mental health or substance abuse issues, see https://www.warmline.org. Survivors of sexual violence can contact the National Sexual Assault Hotline at 800-656-4673 or see https://rainn.org/resources.

FOREWORD

Sinéad the Undying

NEKO CASE

I hadn't listened to Sinéad O'Connor's records since the mid-'90s. Yes, I know how fucked up that sounds, I mean why wouldn't I?! It's really hard to explain, but I'll try.

I was the human demographic *The Lion and the Cobra* was aimed at when it came out in 1987, but I resisted it. Why? Because I was a seventeen-year-old asshole. I hadn't actually heard her music yet, but the hype was deafening, and I took that to be a red flag because I considered myself pretty fucking punk. (I fought hard for that feeling.) I also didn't know yet that I wanted to be in a band, because I was a dumb fuckin' girl and who would be into hearing me play? (Turns out I was not so punk.) I thought I already knew the answer to this question in my soul despite never actually asking it.

I was 24/7 tainted and obsessed with music. It was screaming in my face! But patriarchy is magnificent this way, a perfect predator. It told me without even trying that I would be an idiot for even thinking I could play music, and I had no idea what I wanted outside of a fairly narrow territory I was willing to explore anyway. And yes, I thought I was SUPER open-minded, but *punk* at that time was anything but. It was just more rigid conformity and patriarchy. Luckily, I had a lot of dear friends who were coming out and beginning to openly identify as queer, and something about Sinéad's music was lighting them UP. I thought, *OK, show me these goods. Commence with the Sinéad O'Connor.*

Within the first few seconds of "Jackie" I was trapped forever. She changes character in the middle of the fucking song! Her lower register takes you by the throat like a fist of smoke. Then, without warning, out of that delicious oily witch of a curse she goes straight into the dance club ripper "Mandinka." My little mind was blown. Then, in "Jerusalem" she says she's gonna fucking hit you if "you say that to me." WOMEN WEREN'T SAYING THAT SHIT IN SONGS! Women and their issues with their own violence had no place to even be a thought, let alone be in a song on a massive hit record. It did not escape me. It broke a little something open for me.

By the time "Just Like U Said It Would B" asked "Will you be my lover? Will you be my mama-uh-uh?" I was openly weeping (and not just because somebody finally managed to sing the word *lover* and not make it sound unbearably stinky), because I heard her ask me as me, for me, as a female. It meant so much more than hearing a man ask it in a song—that happened all the time and they didn't fucking mean it! Then I felt the deeper sympathetic crushing (the painful crushing, not the puppy love kind) my friends must have been feeling. I didn't take my queer friends' struggles for granted and I tried hard to be there for them, but I wasn't having to come out for anyone. I wasn't in a music and media desert where no one ever expressed their desire without fear of being shunned, canceled, excommunicated, or beaten to death for using the gender pronouns their hearts wanted to speak. I got a glimpse of how much more loneliness is possible, and how endless and horrible the varieties of neglect were, and I cried harder. I'm still crying about it today.

Back then *nonbinary* hadn't really happened for the fringes, let alone the mainstream, and *trans* was not a term I fully understood. There didn't seem to be any agreed upon terms? But in the song it's irrelevant if O'Connor herself is gay or straight or man or woman or they/them, because she sings it like an avalanche, with passion and abandon and desperation, and she respects herself and respects all of us who could possibly be out there listening so hard to hear even a shred of ourselves in a song. The sacredness of vulnerability and intimacy is more religion than performance here.

One thing I've learned looking up Sinéad O'Connor's career is how little I actually knew. Back then I had to rely on a cassette tape, and her occasional appearances on late night TV. I didn't have cable TV (or any TV really), so I saw her videos from time to time at friends' houses or random places. And in her early videos she's just singing. Which is glorious! Yes! But she also coproduced her first record (and probably her second) and played a ton of instruments! I also could not afford rock mags and there was no internet, so if she ever spoke about songwriting and the instruments used therein, I had no idea. Not a clue. It would have meant so much to so many young people to see that.

Which brings me to her next album, *I Do Not Want What I Haven't Got*, which came out in 1990. "The Emperor's New Clothes" was the second single but is SO much heavier to me than "Nothing Compares 2 U." When I put it on the other day my first thought was, *Can you fucking imagine being in the studio and hearing for the first time the opening count-in of HUGE drums and the rapid-fire staccato of muted guitar together suddenly fall off the cliff and land fully upright, midstride in an upbeat, jangling pop song?! And then Sinéad comes in?!* I imagined myself in that control room and was (you guessed it) bawling.

Those are the moments we all hope for as musicians and engineers and producers. When they happen you feel like you could stop everything and walk out the door full-up and satisfied for the rest of your life. I cried at the mere thought of her possible joy twenty-two years earlier! Haha! I hope to God she felt it, because things like Grammys and Oscars can't do that to you. You can remain at a distance from reviews and awards—from The Feeling you cannot.

Sinéad was a bona fide superstar by the time *I Do Not Want What I Haven't Got* came out. She could have phoned it in and still sold millions of records; instead she's singing (again) about her own life, her own personal violence, and she does not apologize while singing about the rage hormones can put you through, pregnant and otherwise. I'd never heard a woman talk about this let alone SING about it before. I was raised watching biology-free Lawrence Welk with my grandmother for Christ's sake! To my young, congealing, misogynist mind, pregnancy was not cool—it was "evil," terrifying, the end of your life if you were female, and only for religious people. Please keep in mind, I was feral and had no parents. Having a baby in my subconscious mind was abject fucking cruelty; in my conscious mind, it was nothing short of conformity and "giving up." (Yes, I was fucked up.) She stopped me in my tracks. She ruled the world with "Three Babies," a song about how an abortion actually makes her a better mother. It's not a challenge, a threat, or a justification—it just is. I already felt this way, I understood abortion and my own fierce protective nature. I had just never heard anyone say it before, let alone so Grand Canyon–ly beautifully. I had permission to start thinking about not having to hate my own biology, slowly, in little bits. She started that for me. Her lyrics are so personal and often don't rhyme. They hit harder for it—she speaks of the mundane and it breaks you. Out of the gate in "Emperor's New Clothes" she's brutally plainspoken about the realities of a relationship:

If I treated you mean
I really didn't mean to
But you know how it is
And how a pregnancy can change you

She doesn't apologize, nor does she absolve herself of responsibility, and that's where the crushing tenderness lays so softly right behind that tired truth over an unrelenting dance beat. It's fucking perfect, and it's devastating. There is so much respect for the person she is speaking to (and herself) even though they may be in an impossible place. What a love song. It could have ended there and it would still be perfect, but then we wouldn't make it to the line "I will live by my own policies," so . . .

Sinéad O'Connor's music is a gift I received from my persistent, loving friends. What a beautiful state of affairs. Most of us have "given" music to another person at one time or another and likely changed them away from some darker place, or just gave them some fizzy joy? It just never stops amazing me what that transaction can manifest. I think that's why sometimes we don't listen to a favorite life-changing record for years after wearing it out and committing it to muscle memory. It acts as a poultice—a medicine, some feel-good drugs and a Ziploc bag to keep it in for later, when you need it. When you open it again you may not be ready and maybe that's when you need it most. It feels like the reason we stay alive.

For Shuhada

"Heroine"

SHARBARI ZOHRA AHMED

I must confess, I don't know how to pray as a Muslim. I do the ablutions and face East toward Mecca, genuflect, and that's pretty much where you lose me in terms of the physical ritual or recitations. I have been searching for an Islam that aligns with my (occasional and moderate) vodka-swilling, prosciutto-loving, fornicating approach to life. I didn't want to abandon Islam altogether, because I know enough about it to understand that there must be a middle path. The Prophet (Peace Be Upon Him) talks about it directly: "Do good deeds properly, sincerely and moderately. Always adopt a middle, moderate regular course, whereby you will reach your target . . ."

The target he refers to is Paradise. I am American—Bangladeshi by provenance—so I am a sucker for advertising. I have often joked that what Muslims needed was a Western celebrity endorser, preferably white, beloved, noncontroversial, palatable to the delicate white supremacist and Zionist sensibilities that have grown even more visible as of late. Someone pretty, who could shift the public's opinion away from the notion that all of us were brown terrorists bent on murdering and/or converting the goodly Christians and Jews of the world.

They could do this through a series of PSAs and commercials during the Super Bowl or the Oscars. Anytime I thought about this, Britney Spears popped into my head, though she is far from noncontroversial and is oftentimes in a state of undress. That was simply the scale of influence I was envisioning because in her prime, Britney was something to behold and people trusted her. I've always felt that—whilst acknowledging that Muslims, along with nearly every religious group ever created, have committed acts of terrorism in the name of Allah—those of us who did not prescribe to the violent notion of Islamic identity were suffering from negative branding and PR. Because it seems if you can spin and normalize genocide, which the Global North has been doing for generations, you can spin anything to seem positive, even us Muslims. And that is generally where I left it.

Then Sinéad, the infamously lapsed Catholic artist whose lifelong spiritual quest was a very public narrative of genius, pain, mental illness, grief, truth, and courage, decides to, in her own words, "revert" to Islam. The year is 2018 and I have not thought about Sinéad in a long while. Some of her songs are forever living in my Spotify queue. One in particular I listened to more than others because I felt like she was talking about me or to me: "Heroine." In it she mentions shame more than once and returning to the arms of a beloved and trusted divine source, much like the Sufi mystic Jalāl al-Dīn Rumi in his poetry, but without the shame. Sinéad did appear to prescribe to Rumi's admonitions to "Forget safety . . . Destroy your reputation . . . Be notorious."

And then she died. I was sad and felt guilty, like I should have been listening to her new music and following her life. Like I let a friend down, a fellow Muslimah. She was always so willing to be raw and vulnerable. I wanted to—still want to—be like that. I listened to "Heroine"on a loop the day her death was announced. I have always loved the way it opens—with strings and U2's The Edge's dulcet guitar joining them eventually that reminded me of late-day sun glancing off rippling water. Then a very young Sinéad's gloriously melancholic voice comes in, moving me every time with its haunting lyrics and repetition of the word "heroine," as if to say, That's what I am, that's what you are. Be the heroine of your life, if you can get past the shame and be the "chosen one."

I was scared she killed herself—I wouldn't have judged her if she had but I didn't want "pious" people to criticize her. She had lost her son to suicide. I have a son, only one child, and if he died, I am not sure I could exist in this world. It would no longer be recognizable to me. I would be lost, with nothing to anchor me. I wouldn't give a tinker's damn about Allah or what was sacrilegious.

So many people let Sinéad down, starting with her mother, then the religious community she was born into. This slight-boned girl with the powerful voice, huge, watery pools for eyes, and shaven head, which indicates to me that she was not preoccupied with her ethereal beauty, was forever searching for those arms—divine or human—that wouldn't let her fall. So, she reverts to Islam, which seemed bizarre even to me, an albeit reluctant and befuddled but still sort-of Muslim person. But Sinéad, now Shuhada, was never predictable and that was part of her genius.

Her voice, after her death, speaks as a soundbite from a 2023 NPR program: "The word revert, it refers to the idea that if you were to study the Koran, you would realize that you had all—you were a Muslim all your life, and you didn't realize it." NPR's Scott Detrow interviewed Sheikh Umar Al-Qadri, the Chief Imam at the Islamic Centre of Ireland and Sinéad's spiritual advisor and close friend, after Sinéad/Shuhada passed. And I started wondering if perhaps I was a real Muslim and didn't realize it. I will never take hijab, which means modesty, because I don't think I am responsible for the apparent sexual frenzy my hair or boobs will send men into. They need to manage that. But Shuhada covered her head, even though she had no hair. She wanted to be modest in the face of God. It was showing respect. It was not managing the male gaze, I think. I will never know. This is what I glean from what she says in her songs and how she says it and how she lived, with humility and honesty.

What I *do* love about Islam is that a middle path is encouraged, but no middleman is needed to find that faith. It's just you and Allah, in a room, on the subway, at your desk. They are everywhere and you are right there with Them. No physical structure houses Allah. It's a personal, intimate relationship, and that is what drew Sinéad/Shuhada to it. Her friend, Al-Qadri tells us that Islam appealed to her because she could communicate with God directly. Hell, I've been doing that my whole life, I thought. Al-Qadri says, "She loved also the fact that as a Muslim, we believe in the Torah. We believe in the Bible. We believe in Prophet Jesus. We believe in Moses." Check, check, check, double check, I thought. Me too. I like the whole cast, though I think Abraham should have had supervised parental visits when he was with his sons, Ishmael and Isaac. He was not entirely trustworthy.

She was drawn to Islam because she viewed it as expansive; it made sense to her and was now making sense to me. I listen to "Heroine" at least once a week and I am seeing how Islamic it is. It was cowritten with The Edge and recorded in 1986, well before her huge fame. When I reflect on the lyrics, I think, like she said, that she was a Muslim all along.

This connection and the reassuring arms she longs for in the song could be human, but I always chose to interpret it as divine, echoing Rumi's unseen "beloved" who is divine. There is pain, there are mistakes that were made, but take me in, make me whole, "Confessed but you still feel the shame. Bring me into your arms again . . . Touch these eyes with a broken smile . . ." There is hope, however: "The night is long. But the day will come." Could she be talking about the drug? Maybe. Addiction comes in many forms. She left it up to interpretation, just like Islam leaves it up to the individual to decide how they will connect with God or navigate the world as a Muslim.

She didn't kill herself. I think life hastened her death. Her friends said she found some measure of peace in the end, but not enough for her body to shed years of pain and trauma. She was, for me, the perfect celebrity spokesperson for Islam. She did it on her terms and with complete humility and imagination, and as a fun by-product she was completely *unpalatable* to white supremacist sensibilities. She did sway at least this skeptic's heart. I am moved to revisit my relationship with Allah in part because of her, not because she's white (she's Irish so not a colonizer) or pretty (so pretty) but because she was vulnerable, authentic, and unafraid to be unabashedly herself—a true heroine. I just hope she found her way into the Beloved's arms. No one deserves that protection more. Ameen.

When We All Knew They Were All Wrong

"Jackie"

ZOE ZOLBROD

I don't remember where I first heard *The Lion and the Cobra*, but I recall with startling clarity where I heard it the most: in a dilapidated Victorian group house in West Philadelphia where I stayed the summer of 1988, when I was twenty years old and Sinéad O'Connor was twenty-one. My best friend from high school lived there, and I was subletting from one of the seven other people who paid rent. A dozen or more punks, hippies, anarchists, and adjacent sorts who stayed nearby used the house's common spaces, so there was always a group hanging out on the trash-picked couches on the big front porch or around the long table in the kitchen. If a woman walked in and Sinéad's album wasn't already playing on the boom box, it would be soon. The men were resigned to it. They might exchange glances as a cassette of The Fluid's *Clear Black Paper* was popped out and tossed on the pile of political flyers and broken-spine vegetarian cookbooks, but they knew not to fight.

The opening track on *The Lion and the Cobra* is "Jackie," which starts off slow and soft and then builds, no verse-chorus structure providing sips of release. The lyrics tell a ghost story about a widow who refuses to accept the news that her husband was lost at sea, and who paces the shore long after her own death, steadfast in her belief that he will return. The opening bars plucked my spinal cord every time I heard them, even if it was the third time that day. It wasn't the narrative that moved my blood in new directions. The idea of waiting for a man was anathema. Nor was it mostly the goth imagery, much as it flattered the strength of the lust I was starting to own. No, it was anticipation of the way Sinéad's voice broke mid-song from dulcet tones into a howling rebuke, insisting that she knew better than the young men who had come to announce her lover's death.

Other than my friend, I didn't know the women in the house well, but when I look back, our reaction to Sinéad feels collective. In my recollection, every time "Jackie" played we all scream-sang the lines that marked the shift in tone: *You're all wrong, I said, as they stared at the sand.* Because yes, that was it, the revelation that was crystalizing for me. They—the societal mainstream—were all wrong.

I had mostly known this already. I wouldn't have ended up in an anarchist group house if I hadn't. The previous semester I had read bell hooks in my Women's Studies class, learned the term "the white supremacist capitalist patriarchy," gotten A's on my papers. But during the summer of *The Lion and the Cobra*, I internalized this knowledge. Sinéad's voice and her very existence, experienced in a community equally lit by it, watered the seedlings inside me, helped them to grow. My sense of myself and the world was expanding so quickly that my skin felt tight.

What were They wrong about? The list was long, and I added to it each day. I had already known that the United States was using tax dollars to build yet more nuclear weapons when there were already enough to destroy the whole Earth, but that summer I learned more about why that was happening, which was that rich white men got richer from it. Rich men got richer, too, when corporations like Nestlé manipulated people into buying products that were harmful to themselves and the planet. The rich and their bigoted admirers, lovers of hierarchy who didn't notice that someone was standing on their own neck as long as they could punch down, were backed by government enforcers like the Philadelphia Police Department. The PPD had bombed MOVE, a radical Black liberation movement, three years before, killing eleven people and destroying over sixty homes just a mile away from where I sat on the porch openmouthed as people explained the incident to me, how the police had known there were children on the property when they attacked, how five of the kids died.

Some of my new friends organized their lives around protesting these things. They volunteered with Food Not Bombs, marched with bullhorns and signs, chained themselves to fences at munitions factories. But the wrongs most immediately relevant to many of the young women in the house involved society's gendered expectations. We had grown up with the message, conveyed in ways from subtle to overt, that our primary function was to be decorative and pleasing, and that our bodies belonged to the patriarchy. Oh, the excruciating humiliation that came with realizing how we might have played along with that, even been shaped by it. But now we knew better, and we could refuse to comply. The main way we protested was through bodily expression.

We didn't have to be told that Sinéad shaved off her hair in response to her record label's plan to market her as a pretty girl. The attitude she emanated was as recognizable to us as the backs of our hands, the way the sea was to Jackie. One after another, women showed up at the house with shorn heads, rubbing their palms over their stubbly scalps for the sensual pleasure and smiling. In other ways, we were already in sync with Sinéad's style. We marked the fields of our fresh skin with first tattoos and third or fourth piercings. We stomped around in men's cutoff jeans and big black boots, accented with dashes of thrift store lingerie. We let our boobs hang out and the hair under our arms curl sweatily. If people mocked or leered at us on the street, we happily told them off, at least if we were together. One fun part of reclaiming our bodies was having bed-shaking orgasms. We experimented with who could give them to us, and some of the women started charging money for getting men off, exploring whether that could be a way to take ownership.

And we talked, if most often in whispers, about the inverse of all this choice: the rapes, muzzlings, and violences we'd suffered, the times we'd been forced. In 1988 I didn't know about the systematic child abuse and cover-up occurring within the Catholic Church that Sinéad would later protest. But I was starting to understand that what my teenaged cousin had done to me during the years he lived in my childhood home fell into a category with the most serious bodily trespasses. This connection didn't give me clarity. I didn't gain an identity as a victim, or a desire to avenge myself or protect others or even a yearning to experience justice and healing. Instead, the fact lodged somewhere between my mouth and my gut, refusing for decades to go all the way up or down, giving an edge to my opinions.

In my favorite lines from "Jackie," I heard a cry of defiance and empowerment that could be widely applied: *You're all wrong, I said, and they stared at the sand*. Plucked from the rest of the lyrics, this sentence wasn't only an accusation. It also showed the effect of the charge, the way it shut people up. I envisioned the men looking at the ground, cowed, unable from that position to rape, boss, or bomb again. That's the picture Sinéad's voice painted for me the first summer I spent listening to her, as pieces of a worldview clicked into place. When I was twenty, I ignored that the narrator of these lines is a pining ghost, stuck in a loop.

The thrilling defiance of my late teens and early twenties was soon tempered by a weary cynicism. It was hard to keep learning about so many wrongs when awareness itself doesn't right them. It's easier to expect injustices and shrug off the pain of them, rather than to wade into the quagmire to figure out exactly what's going on. For a time, I protected myself by living in a world parallel to the one They controlled. I didn't consume mainstream media or hang out with many people who did, and in the pre-internet era, this was enough to leave me only vaguely aware of the outrage Sinéad provoked by ripping up a photo of the pope on *Saturday Night Live*. Because I was so disdainful of the status quo, I didn't understand the significance of the gesture or the impact the sneering criticism might have had on her, or even why she would choose to appear on a smug network show in the first place. She should just come back to us, to the small rock clubs and sagging porches where I imagined we all agreed that popes were dumb and children should have rights.

It took me until my forties to recognize the bravery Sinéad had shown. In the early 2010s, living a conventional life with a full-time corporate job and two kids at home, I no longer had frequent access to the ecstasy of singing and dancing to the perfect loud music with friends. In my scant free time, I was trying to write about the sexual abuse I had experienced as a child and the scourge of it in general, how society gins up hysteria about boogeymen and looks away from what is actually happening. One day at work I stole a half hour to read yet another revelation about the Catholic Church's cover-up of clerical pedophiles, and then I did a search for Sinéad O'Connor's name, because hadn't she said something about this, way back when? I only barely recalled it.

One click led to another, until there she stood, straight and still on stage at the 1992 Bob Dylan anniversary concert a couple weeks after she had ripped up the photo of the pope. She wore a tailored sky-blue jacket that wouldn't have looked out of place on the executive floor of the office in which I sat twenty years later, although her shaved head would have made her stand out. The sound coming from the audience after Kris Kristofferson introduced her wasn't the expected rolling-wave fizz of applause, but an arrhythmic growl like a broken engine. When I realized the bass notes in the racket were boos, I sat in my cubicle with my hands pressed to my stomach, feeling kicked in my own soft guts. My earlier alignment with Sinéad came rushing back to me. Her music returned to my playlists. *You're all wrong, I said* became a mantra that would go through my head as I took long walks after writing or researching, trying to let myself both feel the pain of the world and rise up from it, tapping into Sinéad's energy so I could lift my head and not stare at the sand.

I have revisited the Sinéad archives periodically since then, learning details about her history and context. But in 1988, I didn't know much about her biography. I didn't need to. The way she used her astounding voice, certain lines from her lyrics, the way she presented herself to the world let me—let us—identify with her impulse to defy a culture that was wrong about so many things and to search out truth for herself. Her first album remains my favorite, and from it the first song, "Jackie," which few people seem to recall when they think of her. The seafaring mood evokes the start of the voyage. We were so young when we set off. So right about so many things, and also naïve.

There was a gathering that first summer at a different group house in the neighborhood. Our gang trooped over and packed the living room. Characteristically, we insisted on hearing Sinéad. When the lonely dirge of "Jackie" broke into the bouncy rhythm of "Mandinka," I and the other young women in the room—like a certain kind of young women everywhere—raised our arms and began dancing ecstatically, launching the party and shaking the floors of the rattrap structure. We didn't care if the whole building came tumbling down. We wanted it to. In those first moments, she made us feel powerful enough not just to stand our ground, but to fly.

Feel No Pain

"Mandinka"

SINÉAD GLEESON

As a child, I detested my name. Frequently, this led to quizzing my parents as to why I'd been burdened with it, but they were unapologetic. Schoolyard jokers rhymed it with *lemonade*. It was a name never found on those A–Z racks of keyrings, even though I always looked. Irish given names had a resurgence in the late twentieth century, after centuries of British colonization had literally beaten the language out of us: nineteenth-century schoolchildren wore a stick (*bata scóir)* around their necks and a scratch was made for each Irish word spoken. Ten scratches equaled a beating. Parents gave their kids English first names.

Growing up, the only Sinéad in the public eye was a children's writer who happened to be the wife of former Irish president Éamon de Valera. I didn't realize until I was much older, my feminism unfurled, that he was responsible for including Article 41.2 in the Irish Constitution, which states that a woman's place is in the home, looking after her family, and not working in the world. Ireland has changed more socially and culturally in the last ten years than the nine decades since that patriarchal constitution. And yet a referendum to remove this article was defeated in early 2024.

Change happens slowly, but when it comes to hard-won rights, especially around gender, we must be careful never to assume that progressiveness is permanent. Social change in Ireland has often been divisive. Conversations around divorce, same-sex marriage, and abortion have been both-sides'd to death, but much of the legislative change occurred because of the work of grassroots organizations, women's groups, and queer movements. Often they were shouted down or dismissed within the Catholic orthodoxy that was Ireland of so many centuries. This was the context from which Sinéad O'Connor emerged. After a culture of silences, cover-ups, and shame.

We had been waiting for her for a long time.

The first time I saw Sinéad sing felt like a hundred doors being thrown open. A European TV music channel played the video of "Mandinka," where Sinéad, clad in big boots and white jacket, played guitar and snarled the lyrics. Light glinted off the guitar's body as she shook and swayed, bald, striking, confident (it seemed) and with lots to say. Someone with my name! Who also looked like no one else. But it was *the voice* that was the most noticeable thing about her. The raucous ululations that climbed a ladder not just of timbre, but of feeling. That low steely note when she confides "I do know Mandinka" was like a confession. I could not figure out how she bent so many moods and emotions around the notes. It had a kind of electricity that only Sinéad could conduct.

"Mandinka" was the second single from *The Lion and the Cobra*, and was released exactly one week before her twenty-first birthday. Most of her female contemporaries in the charts were being handed manufactured music by record companies, while Sinéad was writing, playing on, and producing her own songs. There were so few women in Irish music at that time, and none making a global impact—but here was this twenty-year-old woman taking up space and speaking truth. I didn't understand what the song's title meant, but it didn't matter. *I got it.*

Later, in her memoir, *Rememberings*, she wrote about Alex Haley's seminal book on race, *Roots*, which was adapted for TV. The series mentioned an African tribe, the Mandinka, and it resonated hugely with the singer. "It moved something so deeply in me," she wrote, "I came to emotionally identify with the civil rights movement and slavery, especially given the theocracy I lived in and the oppression in my own home." Sinéad, as a middle-class white Dublin girl had not yet realized her own privilege, but it's very telling that she identified with another culture so far from the experience of growing up Irish, under the iron fist of the Catholic Church. "I do know Mandinka" was a recognition of powerlessness, and of feeling seen.

The 1980s and 1990s in Ireland—decades awash with shame, misogyny, and fear—were a hard place to be a teenage girl. In 1992, I was eligible to vote for the first time, and it was in a referendum about whether a fourteen-year-old pregnant rape victim would be permitted to have an abortion. It felt like pure dystopia, and Sinéad was at the forefront of several of the discussions around this case and reproductive rights. So many of us looked up to her. She was not afraid to take on those who tried to cover up decades of systemic abuse of the most vulnerable. Institutions that had seemed so unshakable for centuries now had Sinéad rattling the gates and demanding answers. Despite being gaslit and undermined, she consistently spoke into, and against, decades of silence, refusing to augment her language or temper her anger. It was fearless. And it later helped many of us find our voices—in creativity, in activism, in politics—because she urged us to not be quiet. Not just for ourselves, but for more marginalized voices. She had been so unswervingly public in her support of AIDS victims, Travelers, the trans community, and people of color. When contraception was still banned in Ireland, everyone remembers a heavily pregnant Sinéad, wearing a T-shirt that said: "WEAR A CONDOM."

I bought *The Lion and the Cobra* and listened to "Mandinka" on repeat. The reference to an African tribe went over my head. As did the allusion to Salome's dance for King Herod, which her mother exploited, for which Salome ultimately felt her talents were misappropriated. It was a clear swipe from Sinéad at her own artistic practice and integrity being pitted against what the record company expected of her. What stood out above every other line in the song was: "I don't know no shame." A frank declaration that was the antithesis of all that had been instilled into Irish women. Every step of the way, we were made to feel shameful about our bodies, our desires, and through history, in the secret pregnancies and the babies born that were forcibly adopted. I did not—and still don't—believe Sinéad when she sang: "I feel no pain," because her own anguish was a microcosm of the entire country's intergenerational trauma. Determined to say the unsayable, and in a country so adept at silences, she was a beacon. She was us, and we were her.

And where to even start with that epic, *ne plus ultra* voice? Sinéad was her own instrument, a medium through which pure emotion moved. Her cathedral of a voice crept under our collective skin, the righteousness of her words lodged in our consciousness. The voice that sang of love and loss, of sedition and inequality, of transcendence and faith. It now feels as though we must use her own songs to mourn her.

I was lucky enough to meet Sinéad a few times, and the last time was after the last shows she ever played in Dublin, in 2019. For the encore, she sang a new song, "Milestones," which ends with the lines:

One day we'll sit with our maker
Discuss over biscuits and soda
which one of you and me was braver
Which one of us was a true soldier?

On stage, her daughter Roisin accompanied her on several songs. Backstage afterward, wearing a hijab, Sinéad was smiling, happy, holding tight to Roisin's arm. In the same venue, five months before she died, she accepted the Choice Music Classic Irish Album award for *I Do Not Want What I Haven't Got*. It was a quintessentially Sinéad appearance, as she used her time to welcome and thank refugees. In the widely shared photos of her clutching the award, she is giving the middle finger, her head wrapped in a keffiyeh in support of the Palestinian people. It's a long road from "Mandinka" to July 26, 2023; a life filled with unforgettable music, generous acts of altruism and activism, alongside many private sorrows.

There was no one braver or more uncompromising than Sinéad O'Connor. An agitator, a seer, a warrior, her too-short life was a lesson in how to be courageous, how to live a generous and politically engaged life, and how to never falter in being who you are. Sinéad was possessed of an incomparable voice, a divine and ethereal phenomenon that she gifted to the world, and we were lucky to have it for the time that we did.

Of Fire and Ash

"Troy"

GINA FRANGELLO

The Vatican tour leader stops at the statue *Laocoön and His Sons*, telling our small group how the Trojan priest Laocoön, depicted in agony with his two children as they are attacked by serpents, was suspicious of the Trojan horse, even sticking it with a spear. For this, the gods sent serpents to kill them, which caused the people of Troy to believe in the legitimacy of the Trojan horse, leading—infamously—to their downfall. Or, says our guide, "If Troy does not fall, we have no Rome."

Historians strongly disagree, considering most of the cast of the Trojan War was made up of "gods" and fictional characters, but standing in Vatican City with the sounds of Rome—*the Eternal City!*—surrounding us, it feels convincing. No Rome without the fall of Troy. No . . . Roman Empire, no Mussolini, no pope? But that isn't what the tour guide means, and not the entirety of what I mean, either, here in 2024 pursuing Italian citizenship with desperate hopes of an escape plan for my children. *Bring on the Trojan horse*, our guide implies. *Let Troy burn.*

We have always been a world of *the ends justify the means.*

In the twilight of 1990, my best friend, Alicia, and I took a road trip to visit my new boyfriend, who would one day become my first husband. We listened to a mixtape, only two songs of which I remember now: "Troy," by Sinéad O'Connor, and "The Beautiful Ones," by Prince, who also wrote "Nothing Compares 2 U," the song that brought O'Connor the most mainstream success of her career.

In my memory, these two songs played on constant loop, echoing the obsessions in my mind: since the last time I'd seen my new boyfriend, a Richie Cunningham type, currently long-distance, I had briefly lived with another man in London, while bartending there under the table. Songs of illicit love (as we then believed "Troy" to be) and of a woman choosing between two men ("The Beautiful Ones") spun me deeper into my sense that, for the first time, my life was the stuff singers pushed their voices toward until something supernatural occurred. I was twenty-two. "I wouldn't have screamed *No, I can't let you go* if the door wasn't closed!" I belted along with O'Connor. My South African lover in London was the one who had "tried," I the one who would "never have known," in some alternate universe where people adhered to church-dictated morals and forgot entirely that they were young and alive and in London for only a fairly short time.

Alicia gave me a look I would recognize in the eyes of some friends twenty-five years later, when I left my long and alternately tumultuous and stifling marriage after a hot and heavy midlife affair—a look that said I needed to get my head out of my ass. "You know," she told me, "you don't have to tell him. You should, absolutely under no circumstances, tell him."

But I did tell my new boyfriend, then and twenty-five years later. For better or worse, as liars go, I have always suffered from an excess of honesty.

I'm in Rome with my youngest child, who is off to college at the end of August. They're a visual artist and wanted to see the Sistine Chapel despite having been a staunch atheist since they were eight, once even getting beaten up by a group of boys in middle school for having made up an antireligion song and singing it insistently, back when they, too, were known as a boy and had to content themself with small rebellions.

Now, a theater major at their performing arts high school, they played Juliet in their annual showcase; in Italy, everyone addresses us as "signoras." My youngest is eighteen, two years younger than O'Connor when *The Lion and the Cobra* was released, on which the intense, tour de force "Troy" appears—though it turns out that song, like the legend of Laocoön, is a shapeshifter. O'Connor wrote "Troy" at seventeen; by twenty, she was pregnant with the first of her four children, one of whom would die by suicide at seventeen, not long before her own death. By 1992, when she was twenty-six, O'Connor had ripped up a photo of Pope John Paul II on *Saturday Night Live*, an act greeted with such vitriolic "canceling" you would have thought the cast of *SNL*, and later the audience at Bob Dylan's thirtieth anniversary concert—which booed her—were comprised of nuns.

The outstanding 2022 documentary, *Nothing Compares*, movingly links O'Connor's lineage of resistance not only to other feminist musicians' but to activists like X González, a survivor of the Parkland massacre. Still, if O'Connor was the sacrifice on the altar to make such lives possible (and why, as Tori Amos sang, does there always "gotta be a sacrifice?"), I long to reach into the past and beg, "Don't throw yourself on the pyre. You will just be dead, and still, they'll be coming for our bodies." I am motherfucking tired of rising from the ashes, and I am a white, cis woman. Two of my three children are people of color, the third gender nonconforming.

My phoenix babies were born into a world already trying to break them.

I was twenty-four in 1992, during the Pope Incident: engaged and suffering from a variety of ailments most doctors then bracketed under the heading "anxiety." My problem was simple: I could not get my breath to hit bottom; my lungs never felt full. My problem was not-so-simple: I was emerging from an eating disorder that had plagued me on and off for a decade; I was engaged to a man who had tried to break up with me three times, each time dissuaded by my efforts to convince him otherwise. My problem was deeper: I was enmeshed in internalized religious and misogynistic fear, brought on by my Catholic education and years as an altar girl, that I was going to hell because I was a slut, even if now I was a reformed slut intent on getting my Richie Cunningham, whom I loved with more than a tinge of desperation, to keep me reformed forever.

My confession to having cheated on him with the South African had been met with considerable grace. When it happened, he had gone home to the States to ready himself for grad school, while I remained behind in London and promptly moved so many times in short succession that none of his letters ever reached me. I believed he had not written, maybe even had reunited with a former fiancée, on whom he admitted he was still somewhat hung up. Thus, when I came clean, we concluded it was not really "cheating." We agreed to this tacitly until, twenty-five-years later, it became an ominous foreboding: an essential character flaw.

I met my 1990 lover, William, thanks to my new job at the Latchmere in Battersea, where a fellow bartender told me of a newly opened bed at a step-above-a-squat called Arthog House. She said she wouldn't mind another girl around the place, which housed eleven men from around the world. I moved into a twin bed with a deeply sloping center, next to gigantic, uncovered windows that caused surprisingly little disturbance to my sleep given the perpetual gray of London. I shared the room with a Kiwi named Graham, though after . . . a week? a few days? . . . I was rarely in it anymore, having moved upstairs with William, with whom I'd had sex in our underground kitchen after pilfering a pound of ground beef from the roomful of residents we didn't know and covering it with every spice we could find. William seemed to think cooking stolen meat for me a romantic act. When he tried to fuck me on the kitchen floor, there didn't seem any reason to resist even though I was in love with the American boy I believed was never writing me again. William shoved the cast iron skillet off the flame; dust and grit stuck to my naked back.

Earlier that night, he'd sat at the Latchmere until closing time so he could offer me a ride home on the handlebars of his bicycle. Thirty-four years later, I can still smell the precise London breeze against my skin and feel the sensation of flying.

The other men called me William's "old lady" and treated me respectfully because I belonged to one of them. We often joked that I was Wendy among the Lost Boys. For years after I settled down, I still dreamt restlessly of flying like Wendy through the window at Arthog House, soaring around the house looking for William. He was home in South Africa by then, living in a rondavel. In a letter he'd written, *We only knew each other for a short time, but you made a big impression.*

I also remember lying on the sofa upstairs with one leg slung round his shoulder as he sat upright, and how he indicated my position and said, "Do you want to get fucked?" I hadn't *thought* that was what my body language meant, but I took his word for it when he put me on my hands and knees. I remember telling my roommate Graham that I was worried my American boyfriend would dump me when I told him about William, and Graham saying, "If he really knows you, he won't be that surprised." I held this like some kind of balm—thinking of it that way for *years*—before it began to feel like a slap.

Sometimes the exact things a young woman interprets as "freedom" are the details that later make the version of her old enough to be her own mother at that time wince.

O'Connor's lyrical admonishment, "You should've left the light on," would come back to me many years later, when I'd have guessed I was long past my "Troy" years. I was a guest writer at the California MFA where the man who became my lover in middle age teaches, when I received news of the sudden death of my surrogate sister. I stayed in his room for comfort; everyone I shared with the deceased was home in Chicago mourning en masse. I spent the night weeping; various colleagues offered red wine, guitar strumming, sedatives. I was still anesthetized in numb disbelief when, one by one, each friend broke off to go to bed, leaving me alone with the man who would become my lover.

Is there any way to explain how, in the throes of grief, my response to turning off the lights to sleep was to all but beg to kiss him? He refused, given my condition, but we spent the night intertwined, electrified, more whispering than screaming "No, I can't let you go!" in the face of our closed door.

Then I wouldn't have tried and you'd never have known

My flight home did not dissolve the spell. Soon, I kissed his face and more. Eventually, I confessed, with some residual Catholic notion that admission by choice would cleanse me. Instead, I was cleaved, burnt down. In the years that followed, there would be a high-conflict divorce, job loss, a bilateral mastectomy and chemo, two dead parents, and three shell-shocked children left standing with me in the ashes.

Makes no difference what you say. You're still a liar.

It was not only my youthful self-absorption that made me misinterpret "Troy" so deeply. At the time, under the collective sway of our semi-newly liberated sexual appetites and women—beautiful women with major record label deals!—singing about them, *Pitchfork* declared that "Troy" painted "the story of desire and betrayal on a wall-sized canvas," and *Slant* said, "the fierce melodrama of young love and betrayal is imbued with the surrounding violence in 'Troy,' the song's crumbling romance equated with the burning of the famous Greek city."

In *Nothing Compares*, however, O'Connor explained that "Troy" was about a period of her youth in which she was forced to live in the garden, begging her mother to allow her in as she watched the light switch off for the night. O'Connor described "Troy" as "not a song, it's a fucking testament." Through this lens, the lyrics seem to alternate between O'Connor's perspective and her imagined mother's, a master class in an abuser's gaslighting, and lend an ominous significance to O'Connor's untimely death. She was not only betrayed by the public, but those betrayals began years prior, were the source wound of the music we laud, pointing our fingers at burial grounds of Native children under Catholic residential schools, at massive sexual abuse cover-ups worldwide, and shouting, "Sinéad was right!"

But *of course, she was right*, no matter how we interpreted the song. Did anyone—and by "anyone," I mean the Boomers at a Dylan show who had once tried to change the world; the audience of *SNL* and its allegedly Dionysian cast, where nothing was supposed to be sacred—think she was wrong even at the time? Was it her perceived "wrongness" that led to the brutal backlash, or something else entirely?

It feels important to note that Cassandra, like Laocoön, predicted the downfall of Troy, but because she wouldn't give Apollo any, he cursed her to never be believed, though he likely needn't have bothered, given she was a woman. Sinéad/Cassandra, twinned oracles, condemned for telling the truth. Sure, yes. Along with millions of women worldwide throughout time, including the so-called post-#metoo era: Juanita Broaddrick, Mariah Billado, Tasha Dixon, Christine Blasey Ford, all the women whose allegations cannot be found on Wikipedia. Justice Sonia Sotomayor, who wrote, "With fear for our Democracy, I dissent."

We are a world lousy with Cassandras.

"Why, what could she have done," W. B. Yeats wrote in "No Second Troy," referring to Helen, "being what she is? Was there another Troy for her to burn?"

And what am I? Is being "a liar" an essential, permanent state, or a transient choice when what holds us down and burns us is misinterpreted as freedom—even as revolution? I'll never answer those questions fully. They'll be with me, the Troy I burn, over and over again until my death. Being what O'Connor was, what she'd endured, by 1992 was it already too late for other outcomes later in her life? (*Very early in my life*, wrote Marguerite Duras, *it was too late . . .*)

Yeats is buried in Ireland, and O'Connor, too, though in a different cemetery, in Dublin, that recollected rainstorm now her eternity.

On our last day in Rome, less than a year after O'Connor's death, my youngest child and I stand in the non-Catholic cemetery, visiting the grave of another immortal, John Keats. Beneath the ancient Pyramid of Cestius, we read Keats's inscription: *Here lies One Whose Name was writ in Water*. Keats believed, at the time of his death, in his eternal obscurity. So, it has become a common refrain that the collective "we" did not appreciate Sinéad O'Connor sufficiently when she was alive. And though her death has been attributed to natural causes, I still can't shake the sense that the Troy so many women burn, in absence of other choices, is our own bodies.

So often, the Trojan horse is coming from inside the house.

Yet in Ireland, in part due to O'Connor's lifelong efforts, the Catholic Church has lost much of its stronghold, a once unimaginable feat. Abortion is legal; sexual abuse cover-ups have been unearthed and apologized for; women are legislatively entitled to equal opportunities; trans rights are more progressive than in the United States. O'Connor has proven that indeed she will return, "the phoenix from the flame."

My youngest's eighteen-year-old body, willowy and pale as Sinéad's, stands tall and strong beside me as we look down at Keats's grave. "Troy" was not "writ in Water" but in fire. Here I am, risen so many times from the flames that I am part ash, grateful to be some crumbling and watery part of women's artistic lineage of dissent.

But my children: the dust still packs firmly beneath their feet. They are only just beginning to regenerate, to fight, to sing.

Open Letters to a Spiritual Soldier

"I Want Your (Hands on Me)"

PORO CHISTA KHAKPOUR

1)

Dear Sinéad,

I am writing you in this way because I've written to you in so many ways, so many times, over so many years, in and out of my head, all over the place—and this is the form I keep coming back to. The word *letter* holds more possibility, is appropriately precarious, more imperfect and hopeful. It's more me, it's more you.

Every few years you would write an open letter which would appear like a blessing, and occasionally a curse . . . and so, I am going to make this as *open* and *letter* as possible, in your honor.

Sinéad, just know we all feel like shams before you, even when you're not here. Maybe more so now? *Sham* is part of how it feels to be your fan. Unworthy, and yet knowing you'd be annoyed at us resorting to the concept of unworthiness, the very complacency of self-hate being probably its most criminal feature.

Dear Sinéad, it's been 369 days and who knows how many hours, and I still feel so lost without you.

2)

Dear Sinéad,

Let me start over: I am writing you this letter because you were one of the greatest loves of my life. And you never knew that. In fact, if you remember me at all, you may remember me as maybe the opposite—a nobody who was briefly on an adversary's team online. A mess! But do I regret that? Sinéad, not really, but I think you'd understand. You wouldn't want me to regret it, that's the wildest part.

You were the exact age I am now, months away from forty-seven—a scraggly unpleasant age, let's be real. I meanwhile was thirty-five, an age that feels official and airbrushed and almost corporate, the perfect adult marker where you don't just think you know everything, you *know.*

I wrote, with so much confidence on 10/17/13, a tweet that still exists: "@SinéadIsClothed Hey Sinéad, you were my hero as a kid! Now you are someone who is harassing my friend! PLEASE STOP. Not okay!"

The next day I sent another: "Are you really Sinéad?! Is this for real? I've been told you are the real deal, but are you THAT reckless?"

The account "SinéadIsClothed" is suspended, and over the years, you had many accounts. I can't recall the exact nature of your insults to me, but you were mad that I was defending someone you had decided was your enemy, at least in the span of this particular discourse, which a friend called #MileyGate.

My friend was seven months pregnant and wasn't even sure why she was fighting Sinéad to defend Miley Cyrus. It wasn't any of our lanes really. I wrote to a man I was dating about how bizarre it was to be berated by my icon of icons, and he wrote back: "I know you are loath to walk away from anything. But please walk away from this one. It's not your dance. And something is wrong with that poor woman."

I remember resenting his condescension, even while it put me back in check: I was with Sinéad again, like I used to be, no fight in sight. We were allies and he was not.

3)

Dear Sinéad,

You first came to me when I was ten. "I Want Your (Hands on Me)" was released as the fourth single from your 1987 *The Lion and the Cobra*. I did not yet know that it would forever be my favorite album of yours. The only other cassette I owned was Madonna's *Like a Virgin*, and I had no idea you two had some odd rivalry or else just didn't like each other or who knows. I was new to America and didn't understand where any of this came from, except that the girls at recess in suburban California had good taste and music was our life. They would fight, too, and I had practice staying out of it. In that run-down dingbat apartment building full of fellow immigrants in the one low income part of our suburb, there was always the sound of fighting, which I would drown out with music. My cheap boom box played my few cassettes; in our living room there was also a tiny TV that somehow aired MTV; we had rides in my mom's old Honda hatchback which was dialed to pop radio.

And so: I found you. Somehow.

You were always a major player in my psyche, from cool girl on the radio to a voice of conscience in our communities to, ultimately, something like kin. There is a way in which every Sinéad O'Connor fan I have ever met feels as though they took you in with the most intimate of alone times. Not raves, not stadiums, not nightclubs—the best way to be a fan was to be alone, maybe even under the covers, in the dark, with the headset of a Walkman hovering over our ears.

I was a writer and I didn't know then that pop stars could be writers, too. Even at age four I knew I wanted to be a writer of anything from books to poems to songs, but I couldn't imagine what that meant in the real world.

You wrote "I Want Your (Hands on Me)" with four other men. Sinéad, I had no idea what it meant to be a feminist then and I swear decades later, wearing a "The Future Is Female" shirt, I probably knew less of being a feminist than I thought. We are a work in progress, especially now, all the more without you. You once called yourself a "female spiritual soldier," and I think that was correct.

4)

Dear Sinéad,

I remember my friends from that time warning me four was an unlucky number, and I look here and see so many number fours. Apologies, Sinéad, our common religion, Islam, should make us above such things, but on nights like this—four a.m.—I retreat into my old fears, wobbly and brittle and yet still so real, like a castle made of cards. Nothing, anything, can blow it all over, when it can be as effortlessly undone as swiftly rebuilt, a tirelessly regenerating fortress of phobias.

Where are you, Sinéad? Why did you go like that?

So many of us would rather be there. I know we don't know, but it can't be that much worse than this. Maybe that's the foolishness of the living. We always think like this. Maybe that alone is how we know we are not ready.

5)

Dear Sinéad,

In 1988, two versions of "I Want Your (Hands on Me)" were released: a street mix and a dance mix. Sinéad, I could not tell you which one I heard first and which one I latched on to, because *street* and *dance* only go together for me.

Sinéad, what I remember most about my first encounter with this song was not you. You introduced me to my first favorite rapper, a woman rapper, before I knew that most rappers were men. My world in the years to come would be all J. J. Fad, Salt-N-Pepa, peaking ultimately with Lil' Kim and Foxy Brown—all because of one Lana Moorer aka MC Lyte.

Dear Sinéad, who would believe a white Irish girl could introduce me to a Black rapper from Brooklyn? In South Pasadena, California, I was far away from both, Ireland's 5,150 miles versus New York's 2,787, and none of it meant a thing to a kid who had not been on a plane since early refugee days escaping war.

6)

Dear Sinéad,

After your death, the *Guardian* featured a roundup of collaborators and friends, and MC Lyte's entry was my favorite:

"I first met Sinéad in this swanky little lounge area of a New York City hotel with Fachtna [Ó Ceallaigh, O'Connor's manager from 1986–90]. . . . They had reached out because they wanted me to appear on the I Want Your Hands on Me remix. I believe the photo on the cover is actually from the day we met. I remember asking: 'Why do you want me?' It turned out it was because of some explicit lyrics that I said in a song, mainly the lyric: 'Shut the fuck up.' She was so intrigued by this young person using this language to get her point across and she wanted me to say the words exactly like that on the remix."

In a *Rolling Stone* interview with Christopher Weingarten, Lyte elaborates a bit more: "She was like, Don't leave that part out. I need you to say that part."

Shut the fuck up.

I need you to say that part.

This made so much sense to me.

In the *Guardian* MC Lyte recalls you in a way we often forget you were: *soft-spoken*. But also "honest and kind." She thinks you gravitated to rappers because you "appreciated the genre for its honesty and for the ability of those in it to speak a language that was not accepted by the mainstream." She says, "Had it been a different time, and if she didn't sing as well as she did, she might have rapped to get her message across."

MC Lyte recalls little moments—playing a game of "it" at the gas station when you went on the road with her. She recalls the simplicity, the joy, and much later, the tearing of the photo of the pope and how gutsy and appropriate it was, that you were so ahead of your time in announcing what everyone was slow to declare. "At least you can rest easy knowing you've said what needed to be said," she says. Sinéad, that broke me.

She talks of "overwhelming sadness" in your absence. But MC Lyte being MC Lyte, she does not end on that note. Instead: "What a powerful force of nature she was. And is. What do you do with that type of energy? She lives on."

When "I Want Your (Hands on Me)" came out, you were twenty-two; Lyte was eighteen.

You were both kids and yet never kids.

Journalist Kathy Iandoli pointed out you both had parallel debuts in 1987: you with your debut album, MC Lyte with her debut single "I Cram to Understand U (Sam)" created at just sixteen years old, written when she was twelve. It was taken as an antidrug song, but also a song about infidelity. Lyte samples herself from that song on her verse in "I Want Your (Hands on Me)."

When I heard you, I recognized something. I was writing novels at single digits, you were writing iconic rap songs. All I wanted was role models with pen and paper. They didn't need to look like me or sound like me—Iran felt like a galaxy away anyway. But there was so much there that I latched on to, precocious young women, the drive of girls who can already tell the odds will be stacked and steep, that the only way is through.

Dear Lana and Sinéad, did they call you child geniuses? Dear God, I was never once called a child genius, never got to be child or genius when I was still negotiating the tangles of existing as an American girl.

In my teens I became a critic, and through my twenties I was a music journalist writing about hip-hop and rock. I mostly wrote about women who were unlike other women. I wrote about collaborations and mash-ups and all the magic you could not define.

I did not have a category myself in this country. I was neither you, Sinéad, nor you, Lana, but I swear there were bits of both of you in me.

For as long as I can recall, I have thought of family as a sisterhood, a lineage of women, matriarchal communities, the ghosts of my grandmothers from their small villages in Iran on the same plane as the rap gods and rock stars of our era. You showed me the way home. A way home. The way?

7)

Dear Sinéad,

For ages, I struggled with the title "I Want Your (Hands on Me)." I could never remember where the parenthesis was or what it meant or how to even say it. I think it's your worst title and yet it's your first song I fell in love with, so it will always feel like my favorite.

I can never remember all the lyrics—because they are so easy, with "put 'em on" repeated almost a hundred times.

But it's "I want your feelings" that sticks with me most.

This is a decidedly pop anthem about yearning, equal parts giving and receiving, sexy and decadent and yet a bit icy and rigid in its expressions of surrender. It's a huge contrast to other hits of that year that were almost rabid in their lusty effusions: George Michael's "Faith," Guns N' Roses' "Sweet Child o' Mine," Billy Ocean's "Get Outta My Dreams, Get Into My Car," U2's "Desire." As for women, radio favored Tiffany and Debbie Gibson, whose vocals were kept surreally doll-like as if dipped in artificial sweetener.

The darkness, edginess, almost ethereal agitation of you and Lyte was something else. In a time when video vixens were all the rage, you were hair metal ballad ingenues and your own main characters, too.

Your music video was mostly just you vibing, in your signature understated cool, sometimes beatifically and sometimes a tad insecurely, unchoreographed and under-rehearsed, over a green screen panel of rotating and revolving flowers interrupted only by disembodied hands. They look like screensaver carousels, as abstract and odd and cheap as they are beautiful and romantic and otherworldly. You in that trademark look of yours: white T-shirt, jeans, black leather jacket, and your ultimate accessory, your shaved head. Your skin is flawless without any real sign of makeup, and you are mostly poker-faced with an occasional small smile and of course that animal gape that could mean wail, bellow, or snarl. You look like everyone's dream queer girlfriend—nothing outdated about you even today—a touch feral while also steadfastly self-possessed, a wayward poet and reluctant professional in accidental "skinbyrd" optics that anyone could fall deep in crush with at least.

And then MC Lyte, who seems the object of your gaze, so young and almost surprised to have a cameo on the song. She looks a bit like the hard femme to your soft butch, and the romance in your lyrics seems almost directed at each other, even though it's clear that you, like the flowers, exist in planes that touch no one and no thing.

Lyte is in a sweatshirt and denim, classic bamboo doorknockers on her ears, crisp American urban cool with a mic in hand.

I'm not the type of girl to put on a show
'cause when i say no, yo i mean no
But when it comes to you
I just can't refuse . . .

I was grounded by Lyte, and mesmerized/disturbed by the rest. The song revolves around the notion of putting your hands on someone or receiving someone's hands on you. At that point in my life to "lay hands on people" was only the negative, or that was what I had picked up, at least, English still something I was trying on. I was a troubled kid in a troubled home, enduring lots of physical abuse from various sources. It would be years before I thought of someone putting their hands on me as exciting, erotic, desirable, or even tolerable.

8)

Dear Sinéad,

In 2013, you wrote your most talked-about open letter, which starts like this:

Dear Miley,
I wasn't going to write this letter, but today I've been dodging phone calls from various newspapers who wished me to remark upon your having said in Rolling Stone your Wrecking Ball video was designed to be similar to the one for Nothing Compares . . .

> *So this is what I need to say . . . And it is said in the spirit of motherliness and with love.*

You continued with language that shocked many of us who refused your sex-negativity and slut-shaming, or even just your use of *pimp* and *prostitute* as pejoratives. Your closing included these lines:

> *You ought be protected as a precious young lady by anyone in your employ and anyone around you, including you. This is a dangerous world. . . .*
>
> *I am happy that I made that choice, not least because I do not find myself on the proverbial rag heap now that I am almost 47 yrs of age . . . which unfortunately many female artists who have based their image around their sexuality, end up on when they reach middle age.*

Days later, an old friend of mine, journalist, screenwriter, and former sex worker Ruth Fowler, penned a response at *CounterPunch*:

> *I hate Open Letters as a rule. There seems to be a fad for them at the moment, as if people in the 21st century aren't quite confident enough to be a douchebag without framing it in a faux epistolary form which feigns a dialogue. People who write Open Letters don't want a dialogue. They don't want a conversation. They don't want a response.*
>
> *They want an audience.*

She said a lot more also and apparently used language that was too harsh for you, language now edited out so I can barely put it all together.

Jeffrey St. Clair, editor of *CounterPunch*, felt compelled to add a note after you contacted him:

Even CounterPunch staffers recoiled at the use of the word "cunt" and the phrase "should probably be kicked in the vagina." Ms. O'Connor contacted me to express her genuine outrage at the essay and the fact she felt the language was an incitement to sexual violence. . . . At her request, I have removed the offensive sentences. We apologize to Sinéad O'Connor, a musician we have long admired and a known victim of sexual violence and to other victims of sexual violence.

And somewhere around this moment, we were all arguing on Twitter, and I interacted with the greatest icon of my life in a manner I did not expect, want, or enjoy.

You meanwhile fixated on responding. It was hard to argue with what you produced:

It is No Measure of Health to be Well Adjusted to a Profoundly Sick Society, you wrote, quoting Krishnamurti.

Is having the close up HD slow fuckin motion face of Gaddafi being shot off on the front page in massive technicolor on all the bottom shelves of news stores so that every child in the universe can see it, sane?

Is that a sane practice? No. Did Britney Spears ever do anything like that? No. She fuckin' didn't.

Because she is a lady, not a whore for blood. She got made crazy by the media when there was fuck all wrong with her BUT the media. She got Kafka'd. . . .

When the afflicted are mocked they die. When their heroes are mocked by their perceived mental afflictions, they die. . . .

Because I'm the type of woman that media wouldn't want being a hero. Because it doesn't suit them to have women feel strong. And so they'll use other women. Who'll write venom about women. Kafka again.

I'm honored to be one in an ancient historic line. Of female spiritual soldiers. . . .

I kept reading it over and over, like it was a code to crack. What stayed with me most was how it ended:

When can crazy stop being a term of abuse?

Sinéad O'Connor *is a musician and activist.*

9)

Dear Sinéad,

I could never watch the *Nightmare on Elm Street* films when I was a kid because they scared me too much—even the commercials scared me. We had serial killers in our city and an Elm Street, too.

But I had to watch when I realized "I Want Your (Hands on Me)" played not just during the ending credits of *A Nightmare on Elm Street 4: The Dream Master* but also during a key character's death.

Debbie Stevens, the sixth and last victim in the movie, is a feisty tomboy, not great at school, a defender of her friends, and into fitness. She was everything I was not.

She seems to be a bully of bullies and hater of anything that could upset the other girls. Of course she has flaws, and we're supposed to pay attention when she kills a cockroach that has landed on her toast. Her most fatal flaw: she seems to be very unsure Freddy is real.

Debbie dies while working out, managing to fall asleep while lifting weights at home. Freddy finds her in her dreams. As she's lifting she says, "I don't believe in you," and he answers with "I believe in you." He pushes the barbell down, and her body begins to break into insect parts. She begins to transform into a cockroach! The floor is coated in the goo of a glue trap, which sticks to her, and she turns more and more cockroach until Freddy finally crushes her.

Dear Sinéad, I think of you thinking of Kafka when I see this scene.

I read later that producer Rachel Talalay had to pay twice as much for your song, and it's included twice in the movie, in the Kafka-esque death scene of a young feminist symbol but also the closing credits, leaving a generation associating Freddy's murderous claws with the beautiful "hands on me" of your chorus.

10)

Dear Sinéad,

In 2005, you were asked about *The Lion and the Cobra,* and why you don't perform the songs much.

"I'm really proud of them. For a little girl to have written some of those songs . . . I wrote my songs as therapy, if you like. I don't go back to it. I don't want to go there emotionally. I haven't paid all this money for therapy for fucking nothing."

11)

Dear Sinéad,

In 2018, you became Shuhada Sadaqat.

Dear Shuhada,

You and I shared many things, it turns out, but perhaps none more poignant than your turn to Islam, during a time when I was deepening my faith as well, when I was questioning so much and embracing even more. I remember how proud I felt when you started talking of Muslim prayer, wearing hijab, reciting Quran, of the endless possibilities of our faith.

As a Muslim woman what would you say of our current crises? As a human? I know of course. October 7 was just over two months after you passed, and maybe it's good that you didn't see the aftermath and the aftermath of the aftermath endlessly playing daily with no end in sight.

On July 27, 2023, journalist Isabel Debre wrote for The Associated Press:

> *Death threats forced Irish pop singer Sinéad O'Connor to call off a peace concert in Jerusalem in the summer of 1997. At the time, a young man named Itamar Ben-Gvir took credit for the campaign against her.*
>
> *Today, he is Israel's national security minister.*
>
> *The transformation of Ben-Gvir from a fringe Israeli extremist trying to take down O'Connor's coexistence-themed concert to a powerful minister overseeing the Israeli police force reflects the dramatic rise of Israel's far-right.*

You wrote your most important open letter then, to Ben-Gvir: "God does not reward those who bring terror to children of the world, so you have succeeded in nothing but your soul's failure."

12)

Dear Sinéad,

I lost you and then suddenly I lost Lyte. Her not so literally, thank heavens, but at some point in the composition of this essay, I thought to speak to her. I reached out to her management and they arranged for us to talk. After many emails and texts, I got several minutes with her on the phone—her rep texting me we only had a few minutes more than once—while Lana/Lyte—she was fine with both, she said—spoke with the same ease, grace, and confidence I remember from every song of hers. On a midweek afternoon in one of the hottest summer days of 2024, I thought with so much awe and reverence, as she patiently traversed various memories, how did I get here?

Sinéad.

Rewind: I lost you and then suddenly I lost Lyte. In all my years as a journalist I have never had a conversation not record. And then this one somehow did not, no audio registering on my device. No one could figure out what went wrong. I tried desperately the rest of the day to retrieve it and to put to paper what I remembered of our call—one of the most important calls of my life, a childhood idol.

She spoke about working with you like a professional. She spoke about remembering you with gentle admiration. She seemed touched that for me her lyrics were the centerpiece of "I Want Your (Hands on Me)." She was appreciative and quite aware of the impact she had made, that you had made, and that you both had made together. More than anything, I remember her speaking of her devotion to God, what her life looks like most these days, how choosing her spiritual life was just as profound to her as her choosing art.

I remember her agreeing with me that the one mercy within your loss was your strong connection with God in your last era on the planet.

Loss. Then losing that. After losing you. I tried to reconnect with Lyte's rep, but no answer—maybe it was for the best. Like so many strange miracles, sometimes all that is left is the knowledge that the sacred is the immaterial. The flicker of faith's transience; gaps in collective memory; forever lost words; the body in transit; the negative space of the spirit world; the inevitable exit of idols from our planes of existence.

One night, I found it. I wasn't looking for anything, but it came to me, in a season of loss, where I was starving for anything found. It was a sentence, one that brings all these thousands of words to a point of clarity, at least for me. Below the YouTube video of "I Want Your (Hands on Me)," someone named nualamartyn4918 put it so well: "She was the gospel singer for those who have lost faith in almost everything." This is maybe the most perfect definition of you I've ever come across.

Sinéad, I am still holding on. Because you left us, we have to hold on all the more. I feel you in every movement, every question of ethics, every moral twilight zone, ever forked road in the journey of the soul, every loss in a season of incalculable losses (is that every season, dear God?). "For those who have lost faith in almost everything." It's the almost. Our work is still not done, but a part of me is just consoled that yours finally was.

Listen to the Man at the Liquor Store

"Drink Before the War"

MILLICENT SOURIS

I can't get past the men, can you? Does the word *patriarchy* roll off the ears without impact anymore? I'm not sure, maybe it signals who I am more than who and what it is and how it affects us. We live in a world of men, that's a fact, and I attribute acts of war to them. I don't have another structure to compare this to. Men are the architects for the tyranny of the world in which we reside.

> *Somebody cut out your eyes, you refuse to see,*
> *Ah, somebody cut out your heart, you refuse to feel.*

Sinéad O'Connor's song "Drink Before the War" was one of three songs from her 1985 demo to make the cut for her 1987 debut *The Lion and the Cobra*. In her memoir *Rememberings*, she writes: "I'd written ('Drink Before the War') the previous year about my constipated headmaster who hated me making music and campaigned for my father not to let me take my guitar with me back to boarding school, despite the fact that all I could do was make music."

Sinéad attended a series of Catholic schools as a teenager. Previous to that boarding school, she was sent to An Grianán Training Centre in Dublin, run by the Order of Our Lady of Charity in Waterford, Ireland. The Catholics, they do know how to string together some seemingly insipid words for their controlling, abusive institutions to obscure their power, corruption, and lies. Her father paid to send her there, for "rehabilitation," oblivious it was one of the infamous Magdalene Laundries. These laundries, in existence from the eighteenth to the late twentieth century, were under the governance of both the state and the Catholic Church and run by nuns on the ground. They were places for "fallen" women to be sent, by family, the state, the police, hospitals, the Church, anyone in a role of power.

Girls and women were placed against their will in these for-profit businesses to live and work in squalor; they were imprisoned. Typically a fallen woman was someone pregnant out of wedlock or a sex worker, but really any inconvenient female could be sent there, for being poor, mentally ill, physically disabled, abused, or "too pretty." Once placed, these women generally stayed until death, uncared for and often physically and sexually abused. If they did leave a facility, it was penniless, with just the clothing on their backs.

Sinéad shoplifted a pair of silver boots to wear to a concert. She spent eighteen months at the training center.

In a 2013 interview with *Irish Central*, Sinéad talks about her time at An Grianán Training Centre when she was just fourteen:

"It was a prison. We didn't see our families, we were locked in, cut off from life, deprived of a normal childhood. We were told we were there because we were bad people. Some of the girls had been raped at home and not believed. . . . My worried dad thought he was doing the right thing by sending me to be rehabilitated. He told me he even paid for the privilege of doing so. He thought he was doing the right thing.

He was convinced into it. He paid them to take me. I never told him the truth of how bad it was."

For all their purported godliness, the Magdalene Laundries were not. They kept women against their will, forcing them to live in unsanitary conditions, without care or respect, malnourished, and to work without pay. If they bore children, they were taken from them. Many infants born in these facilities were adopted, some sent to the United States. In 2021, after years of investigation, Ireland's Commission on Mother and Baby Homes issued a report asserting that about 9,000 babies and children had died in the eighteen institutions subject to the investigation. At the site of one former home run by Catholic nuns of the Bon Secours order, near Galway, an independent researcher discovered that the deaths of almost 800 infants were unaccounted for, and the details of their burial unknown. Excavation at the site later revealed an unspecified number of human remains. To a modern person these laundries seem like institutions that would have closed a century ago, something out of Dickens. The last one, the Waterford center where Sinéad was sent, closed in September of 1996.

Most facilities had a rule of silence. Women were stripped of their clothes upon arrival and given drab smocks to wear. Punishment came in many forms. Women were beaten and raped, food was withheld, and their heads were shaved. The Waterford Laundry no longer functioned as a business but still housed older women on-site, separated from the girls. The same spirit of abuse dominated the place.

"As a punishment, I would be sent up to bed early to go sleep with the dying old Magdalene ladies. There would be about six of them in the room and me and I was terrified. These women were old and dying and I was scared there."

You say "Oh, I'm not afraid, it can't happen to me
I've lived my life as a good man."

Being good means the rules have been followed, the status quo has been maintained. How many people in the church, the government, how many police officers, doctors, parents, teachers, sent women to the Laundries to protect society and then felt like they did the right thing?

"Oh, no you're out of your mind
It won't happen to me
'Cause I've carried my weight and I've been a strong man."

Carrying your weight means you didn't ask for anything from anybody, you didn't need any help, you were never a burden. Being a strong man, that's the very ideal of masculinity. When I talk about the patriarchy, I'm talking about the maintenance of power achieved by the generational throughline of male-dominated governments, churches, and administrations. The gender of the person who does this work is irrelevant, they are pawns to power, they follow the rules.

The intense abuse Sinéad suffered at the hands of her mother and the Church is well documented, as is the rampant sexual abuse within the Catholic Church. I never forget it was her mother's picture of Pope John Paul II that Sinéad ripped up in 1992, more than a decade before the *Boston Globe*'s 2002 reporting on the Catholic Church abuse scandal involving 4,000 priests over decades and the revelations about the rampant systematic abuse since. She took that picture off her mother's wall after her death in a car accident when Sinéad was eighteen years old. She didn't know what she was going to do with the picture, but she knew it had a purpose. She carried it for seven years until that purpose was realized.

And you live in a shell
You create your own hell
You live in the past and talk about war

"Drink Before the War" is a blues song, not because of any chord progression, but because Sinéad sees the world for what it is and laments its hypocrites. She is a wary, world-wise narrator, a seer who understands how the world is constructed and organized and how it manipulates. "Drink Before the War" is a protest song, an outcry against this uncaring, self-righteous world where the past and its glory are permanent. Assimilation is compulsory. The payoff is just as underwhelming as proper society. We need the man at the liquor store, to dull the senses. One drink, a few, whatever we need to continue this apathy, whatever we need to keep doing this.

Sinéad exploded, like a star, like a supernova. She survived her own imploding, over and over and over again, in a spotlight antithetical to her essence and ethos. Either she was too bright for it, or it was too public for her. She told us exactly who she was, so often and didn't seem to fear anything. Rather, she didn't allow fear to hold her back. Maybe because she had already been through hell, there was nothing left to lose. Or so she thought.

When I was younger, Sinéad's public expression of her vulnerability terrified me; her honesty was painfully bold, something we punished her for, repeatedly. She was a walking live wire, she put herself out there repeatedly, without a safety net.

Then, I never believed there was any strength in vulnerability. I thought it made me weak, opening myself up for pain and scrutiny, without realizing that pain already exists whether I acknowledge it or not. And it will make itself known. Scrutiny is inescapable, this is a damned if you do, damned if you don't kind of world. Now I understand the will, the utter conviction, it takes to be vulnerable. I know that the reed bends and the brick breaks, it crumbles.

The Lion and the Cobra came at the perfect time for my teenaged ears and mind. I drove so many country roads, screaming the lyrics to every single song, smoking Marlboro Reds, getting lost after school to disappear for a bit. And that, that was it? I moved on from anything so expressive, sensitive, stereotypically female with its feelings and demands. I just listened to her alone, never with anyone else. That kind of catharsis was, and still is, private. I tried to find myself in other music, the way we do when we're young, to find who we are, who we envision and hope ourselves to be, who we dare to be.

I come from a family of tough women, just suck it up and don't complain. We are not the squeaky wheels. I live in a fat body; my failures, according to society, are on display all the time. I am always coming from a deficit. So I've always tried to be above reproach, to make up for my body. No one growing up was shy about this grievous error of mine—the world, my family, their friends, kids at school. I couldn't afford to have such liabilities as emotions and needs. I had to find a way to be worthwhile since I failed at being desired, the most important thing a female could be.

Somebody cut out your eyes, you refuse to see.
Somebody cut out your heart, you refuse to feel.

So I became hard. Nothing could touch me. I tried to be in control the entire time, with a great cost to me and no one else.

This became my mindset for most of my life. I carried my weight, I was good, and I was definitely strong. I have a great work ethic, common sense, and reason. I didn't ask for anything. I didn't rage, I didn't cry, I didn't yell. I became the subject in the song, nothing affected me. It couldn't, or I wouldn't be able to keep going. This wasn't just me thinking this was the way it had to be, this was me knowing this was the way it had to be. So I did listen to the man at the liquor store. I used alcohol to both cope and enable some sort of carefree nature, to escape and still stay in control, a life of contradictions.

I read everything I could about Sinéad in the days following her death and watched many interviews. I do this when someone impactful passes, as if I can fill myself up with their words, images, and music so that I won't miss them. It doesn't work, but still I try. She saw and knew the true struggle in this world from an early age, she was committed to it. Our true struggle is the People versus the Empire, this is the basis of every fight, then and now, every movement, every struggle for liberation is connected, the fight is the same. None of us are free unless all of us are free. Hopefully this statement also doesn't fall off the ears.

I have unintentionally served the patriarchy for most of my life by refusing to be sensitive, loud, open, expressive. It wasn't that I followed the rules and didn't ask questions, rather that I refused to be truly human, to fully be myself and to want more from this world for myself. But there's a fine line between protecting oneself, or thinking you are, and maintaining the powers that be. It's something I just can't do anymore.

Bindaas

"Feel So Different"

MADHUSHREE GHOSH

You told me how different I was. So amazing. Such a bindaas girl. Carefree. Independent. Bindaas.

In graduate school, you're the most handsome one in our group. It is 1996—we are in College Park, Maryland. You are the only one among us desi students who has a job with a W2 and a car that works.

"Oh, Bengali!" you say, mock impressed.

A Bengali to you means overeducated, feminist, literary . . . a snob. Your face says so. You roll your eyes, you're derisive. But your soft smile tells me I can change your mind.

I lean into my Bengaliness. "Yes, I am. So?"

"I like Bengalis," you say, shrugging like it doesn't matter either way.

When you speak Hindi, you don't have a South Indian accent. It's unexpected. I like it.

And even though I don't react outwardly, in my heart, I smile. I like that you, a South Indian, like Bengalis.

I will make you love me.

I thought that nothing would change me
I was not listening anymore

It is 1988. Bruce Springsteen is in New Delhi. It is my eighteenth birthday. My mother is being prepared for a hysterectomy. Delhi University campus is empty. Every college student who has some money and knows Western music is at the concert. Didi, my only sibling, the other daughter older than me by three years, and I—we don't even ask Baba for money to pay for the tickets. We know what the answer will be, so why bother. I am wearing a khadi-silk kurta and green salwar with gold threads. The green dupatta covers my nonexistent breasts. I feel like an adult.

Didi and I change three buses to get to the hospital. We take the steps because we are afraid to take the elevator, which may break down and trap us inside. The nurses bustle around. Beeps and hums of medical equipment with a strong smell of disinfectant permeate the entire hallway.

In her room, Ma sits on the bed, a threadbare gown covering her now-ailing body. Waving at the dinner tray, she looks at me, "Ki, hungry? Eat, eat!" She pushes the sad food toward me.

I am eighteen. I am perpetually hungry. I eat. Then Didi and I fight over the limp vanilla cake slice with melted icing. We laugh and crack jokes that only teens find funny.

Ma watches us, her eyes worried and her mind a thousand miles away. The surgery will be tomorrow. She has no need for her daughters' mirth. She forgets to wish me well on my birthday.

Back from work, Baba heads toward the couch across from Ma's bed. They don't say anything to each other. After all, what is there to say?

We are quiet. Didi and I put the tray back. We are quiet.

Before we leave, I wave at Ma and say, "Enjoy tomorrow," like it's a joke.

She smiles because she knows I'm trying to make her feel better.

"I won't be a woman after tomorrow," she whispers.

Only I hear her.

That evening Baba drives, focusing on the road rather than on us. I play with my dupatta's green tassels. I wonder which girl Springsteen pulled up to dance with him when he played "Dancing in the Dark." Later, the newspapers tell us that it's a girl with short hair like Courteney Cox's. Only, she's Indian. Her jeans are designer. She knows how to dance with the Boss.

At eighteen, everyone considers me an adult. A woman.

I adjust my dupatta.

I feel so different.

By the time Sinéad comes on the desi scene, everyone already loves Springsteen, the Beatles, Tull, or Floyd. Maybe U2. After all, who could love a bald white girl?

Her voice makes me falter. I feel her singing with her tears. I feel. I don't share that. People will think I am crazy.

Later, people think she is. Especially when she speaks the truth.

I am twenty when I first hear her voice. The song "Feel So Different" is just that: different. Is she talking about her lover? Or God? Or just her former self? She has secrets in her dark eyes that everyone finds fascinating, but everyone loves a bindaas girl. Not love, like to behold. But to love, like love a caged panther.

My school and then college friends ask, "Who's your favorite singer?"

It's easy to say, "Usha Uthup," or "Sheila Chandra"—safe desi musicians who are different, so no one raises an eyebrow. They still fit in. But Sinéad fascinates me. How do I say that when I should recommend John Lennon? Or even Bruce?

I usually shrug and shake my head. All of them, I say when they insist. I like all the usuals. The usuals.

But now I feel so different
I feel so different

How do I explain to my friends, her eyes look like they search the world for sanity? How do I explain, I feel like the outlier she tells the world she is? How do I tell these Catholic schoolgirls that I, a nonbeliever, feel her Catholic unrest? I don't know her. I am desi. A brown girl. This singer speaks in an accent so difficult to fathom. This girl has her head shorn—what we would do in the olden days if we were widows. Or when parents die, and the boys of the family shave their heads to show their loss, their grief. My hair is what makes me look like a girl. Long braid reaching beyond my backside. How do I explain, this long-haired desi feels for this Catholic girl who is hurting.

I don't.

When they ask again, I say, "Maybe Madonna? Definitely Lennon."

If I tell the girls I know the Western music greats, then I am not the weirdo, the outlier.

I feel so different

By the time she tears the pope's photo, by the time her CDs get bulldozed by angry Catholics, I am in America, homesick, alone, yearning to belong. I shake my head in horror, watching the *SNL* clip, after all, I am from a Catholic school myself. The pope did no wrong, did he? Not that I am religious, but even *I* tell Sinéad, "Why, what's wrong with you?" much like I feel like telling myself, "Why, what's wrong with you?" when I cry for my home while I study in a cold New York for a degree I don't know I want.

When I meet you, I am twenty-four. I am ready to conform. I am ready to be the cool girl who's also an amazing girlfriend. When you say, you're amazing, Madhu—you have shortened my name because you can—I believe you. I want to show off my amazingness. I am an adult. I am an outlier, but not too much of an outlier, not too bindaas.

You like Hindi music. You don't like "Western" songs. I reduce myself.

I thought that nothing would change me
I was not listening anymore

I rarely play Sinéad. I've downgraded to a nonconfrontational Enya. It's easier to conform.

Over the years, I lose my friends. Some from school. Some from college. Some from graduate school. I conform because you like it like that. It's easier not to hang out with male friends—I'm not a slut. It's easier not to be with my women friends—I'm not a lesbian. It's easier to be with your family. It's just easier.

I was not thinking anymore
Although I said I still was

With that, I hold on to you. Through a decades-long marriage. Through my parents dying. Through your job losses. Through your needs.

And I have always loved you
Oh, you have taught me plenty

I'm not bindaas. I conform.

Sometimes, Sinéad appears online. Once to explain mental health. Once to say she's now a practicing Muslim. Once to tell us that she was having a breakdown. Sometimes she sings. Sometimes her words make sense.

I am trying to save my marriage. I pay her no heed.

I am not bindaas. I conform.

Baba used to say, "You can't hold the river in a cup," and he's right.

By the time you and I finally let go of the string that we used to bind ourselves together, I am unmoored. I have conformed for so long, I don't remember how to be anything else.

But then, if you are different, you can't unlearn that, either, can you?

The last time I see you, we are in the courthouse. You press your eyelids hard to squeeze the tears into forming. You show me how devastated you are. I watch you like I would a slide under a microscope.

That day I get my freedom. I have no idea. Instead, I watch you, feeling sadness, the loss of what we could have been.

When you fight me in divorce court, my friends tell me, "Be angry, be mad. You earned it."

But I don't. I am sad. I tried to conform. I cannot.

I should have hatred for you
But I do not have any

It's been a decade since I have seen you. When friends ask me where you are, I say, I don't know but I wish him well. I say that because it's true. I don't want to see you. Have I changed? It must be.

These days I spend hours in the backyard growing greens like Baba used to in India. Beans, eggplant, pumpkins, spinach. I'm harvesting papayas from the tree I planted during the pandemic. I am back to doing what I liked to before I met you. Mostly I live in a house that is silent, just like I like it.

And sometimes, when I am in the mood to celebrate this life I have created, an outlier's world, I play Sinéad.

I wish her well. Wherever she may be.

The whole time
I'd never seen
All I need was inside me

Keen and Keen

"I Am Stretched on Your Grave"

HEIDI CZERWIEC

Keen and *keen* are unrelated at the root. The Gaelic *keen*, from *ceanogh*, lives in lament, a wail beyond words, grief in its most visceral form, literally, as though a keen blade has cut you to the gut. The English *keen* grows out of *ken*, a knowledge born of experience, so that you *can*, a way of knowing, grown so sharp it hones you keen.

"I Am Stretched on Your Grave," a seventeenth-century Gaelic keen, was translated in a moment of resistance as an act of Irish nationalism in the early twentieth century by Frank O'Connor (no relation), an anti-treaty IRA man and friend of Yeats, and set to music by Philip King in 1979 during a period of keen violence in The Troubles. In first-person, a man keens for his dead beloved, refusing to leave her grave, pledging to *lie there forever*.

Sinéad O'Connor's cover of it in 1990 (near the end of Ireland's Troubles but not of hers) stretches back into that history of resistance, carries it forward. Through the song, pronouns unchanged unlike her Prince cover, she stretches on the grave of her personal history, mourning the loss of her youth to beatings and sexual abuse—*My grief for the girl / That I loved as a child*—and swears to her child-self *I still would be your shelter.*

There's a lot I mourn about my own youth. Those who are sharp have grown so through experience, by necessity.

She makes the resistance contemporary, stretching the ancient to meet the modern moment. As a baby Goth, I first was drawn to her fierce rendition at a time when medieval music was widely sampled and mimicked—Enigma's "Sadeness Part II" and its Gregorian chants, Anonymous 4's plainsongs, Loreena McKennitt's "Mummer's Dance," O'Connor's reviled countrywoman Enya, and even Dead Can Dance's own cover of this song. Yet Sinéad keened its plaintive a cappella melody against a classic hip-hop sample of Clyde Stubblefield's beats from "Funky Drummer."

A terrible beauty is born, keen, stretched thin as a drum.

Tragically, this song comes to embody the keen—a resistance to dignified mourning, to restraint, *with tears hot and wild*—after her beloved son Shane slipped his restraints and escaped the hospital where he'd been on watch *When my family thinks / That I'm safe in my bed*. Watched as he slipped beyond. Grief beyond our ken, *night we were lost*, both of them.

Sinéad died eighteen months later, spent that time stretched on the grave of his memory, keening without restraint on social media:

#lostmy17yrOldSonToSuicidein2022 Been living as undead night creature since.

The priest and the friars / Approach me with dread /
For I smell of the earth

He was the love of my life, the lamp of my soul.

My apple tree, my brightness

We were one soul in two halves.

I'd be sure we'd not sever

He was the only person who ever loved me unconditionally.
I am lost in the bardo without him.

with you in your cold grave / I cannot sleep warm

Troubles result when Gaelic and English collide. What else can be when the system fails, when this keen grief eats of the Tree, knows in its bones that birth and pain are now bound, that parting doesn't end at parturition? When I first heard of her death—and later, how—I was breathless, it was no stretch for me, no longer a baby Goth but a mother to a son myself, to connect her most final tweets to this song. Death is the mother of all beauty, but sometimes mothering finds beauty in death, when language itself fails and her keening cannot bring him back, but her broken body is breathless to join him. *If your hands were in mine—*

Her longing to join hands grown so keen it cannot be resisted, a keen past ken, past can, until she can no longer.

I've decided to follow my son. There is no point living without
him.

It's time we were together.

Bringing You Closer to Me

"Three Babies"

BROOKE CHAMPAGNE

FIRST

During the procedure, the sound of the electric pump's suction reminded me of the carnival ride that runs a hilly track in circles, the Tumble Bug. A crank, a low grind: something was about to get going. Only the opposite. It felt like the doctor was churning butter inside me. Or un-churning? All these clashing metaphors emerged fully formed. Acts of creation, during an act of un-creation.

I closed my eyes and willed away the metaphors. This would never become a story. I would not commit the clinic's beige walls and fluorescent lighting to memory. I'd complete this last semester of undergrad, go to graduate school, and write anything but this.

After the black-magical appearance of the plus sign on the stick, though, I would almost immediately scour the internet to read about it. I searched Yahoo! for "celebrity abortions"—not many hits in 2002—and clung to what Sinéad O'Connor said about hers in *Spin* magazine over a decade earlier: "I was very distraught; it wasn't a decision that I made lightly, or that anyone makes lightly." Sinéad O'Connor was a poet, punk, and iconoclast who infused her music with the sadness and redemption of surviving years of child abuse. Through her songs, she convinced herself, and fans like me, that most global issues could be solved through the love and protection of children. She staked her career—her life—on righting these wrongs.

Despite her abuses, or perhaps because of them, Sinéad did not abort her first pregnancy. Years before that *Spin* interview, Sinéad became pregnant in her early twenties at the cusp, like me, of artistic opportunity (granted, hers was a much larger cusp). Her first studio album, *The Lion and the Cobra,* was set to launch weeks after her due date, so her producer Nigel Grainge advised her to get an abortion. She cried, and didn't go through with it. Fourteen years later, I'd just opened my letter of acceptance to graduate school for creative writing. I cried, and I did.

What distressed me most, initially, was my certainty that an action to which I'd never given thought was now the only option. A condom had broken. This guy I'd been dating was a senior year, shoulder shrug of a relationship. We were not in love. We'd never choose to make a future together when we barely wanted the present we were half-heartedly sharing.

But it was okay. "It"—I'd call it nothing but "it"—was simply a procedure, the careful extraction of a Jenga block from the tower I was building toward my future. I'd place this arbitrary block at the top of the structure and forget about it. Other crucial, yet-to-be-realized blocks would serve as my foundation: graduate school acceptance, the desire to find someone to love and an enduring reason to write. Those blocks would prevent the structure from toppling so I could win the game, which was my life.

Once it was over, a nurse led me to the lobby where my first-trimester boyfriend waited with a Smoothie King Immune Builder. I imagined the temerity of wearing an ironic T-shirt like the one Sinéad sported in her third-trimester sphericity. Her belly poked out from underneath a tiny shirt that read WEAR A CONDOM. My shirt would read, "I had an abortion, and all I got was this smoothie."

My boyfriend, whose days as my boyfriend were numbered, rushed us through a sparse crowd of protesters he called "Jesus freaks." I turned his rebuke into a lullaby, singing softly the obvious next line, "out in the stree-eeets." I loved Elton John, but "Tiny Dancer" didn't feel right. Though I lacked the voice and will to sing it aloud, I craved the clash of metaphors in Sinéad's "Three Babies."

I'd been re-listening to Sinéad's *I Do Not Want What I Haven't Got* since I'd read her *Spin* interview, and it was odd that it wasn't her song about abortion that evoked a visceral reaction, but the one about her miscarriages. It wasn't the ostensible story of "Three Babies" but the sounds made within it that matched how I felt driving home from the clinic. The opening guitar strings are overtightened, almost scratchy, and her voice sounds like it's coming from the end of a long tunnel. Her tone starts off gently, tentatively, with a pause before deciding what to compare herself to: "of course / I'm like a [long pause] wild horse." That timid mood ends with the line "the thing that I've chosen to be." After that, her voice rises to an otherworldly, near-holy falsetto when she describes the longing for her dead babies "in my soul / my blood and my bones." Her vocalization is unbounded for the next minute, and her metaphors match her sounds, an almost plaintive whinny. Then she suddenly screams that she's no longer mad like that horse, "still wild / but not lost," before returning to a near-whisper.

"Three Babies" read to me then as purely a testament to experiencing and recovering from loss. In having an abortion, I'd lost something (a baby? a possibility?) of my own volition. But could I lose what I hadn't wanted? In my silence around this abortion, Sinéad's verses sang all my tenors of grief: angry, wistful, confused, questioning. Because her voice expressed every possible emotion, it allowed me—at least in the immediate aftermath—to feel them for myself.

SECOND

Early in my pregnancy that June of 2018, visiting New York City with my husband and daughter, a rat scurried onto the B train to the soundtrack of strangers' screams, and I felt a record scratch in my lower abdomen. On my subway seat, I wrapped my two-year-old daughter protectively around my belly, but a separate, unnameable something persisted inside of it. A reversed torquing, and a memory: what years ago I'd imagined as the unmaking of butter. Not butter melting, that'd be too soft. Only as if the butter had somehow never been? I wanted to stop doing what I always do when I'm scared, which is conjure metaphors. I wanted to reach our destination: to stroll in sunny Central Park with my family, all three of us. All *four* of us. Well, we were on our way to four. But when we arrived, a half-drunk, black-lipsticked clown proffered my daughter a light pink balloon animal. Its tail popped as soon as she touched it, then in the bathroom, I pissed that exact light pink color.

A few mornings later, back home in Alabama, I woke early to the news that Anthony Bourdain had died by suicide. While I read, the butter officially unmade itself in my lower abdomen. Or was it an egg unscrambling? So many analogies to describe a thing as common as song or rain. I waited until the lower half of my body looked like a crime scene before crossing to the bathroom and acknowledging the reality of this miscarriage. A low-level anxiety began to roil: two losses could only be followed by some ominous third. I vowed not to commit to memory the clump of blood in the toilet. I closed my eyes as I flushed.

Triaphilia is the clinical term for the superstitious fear of a "loss of three," and once I learned it, I began the rational exercise of attempting to dispel it. I resolved to simply feel my feelings. I'd lost the baby, the world lost Bourdain, one of my heroes, and this was difficult enough to endure without anticipating another tragedy. For the first time since my abortion, I considered how the way someone has died, rightly or wrongly, affects how I grieve them. Did Bourdain's choice to die mean mourners should more willingly accept his death? Or rather, despite his battles with mental illness and its attendant agonies, did we resent him for it? This miscarriage offered me, I understood, something my abortion hadn't: the balm of a sanctioned sadness. Yet the moral of every abortion story includes the implicit, vital thesis, "Thank God I had a choice!" Examining these disparities brought about more questions than answers. I'd successfully repressed them, until now.

When Sinéad died in the summer of 2023, I was heartbroken, but wasn't sure whether I should be angry. Had she ended her own life? The circumstances wouldn't be known for months, and her recent words presented conflicting evidence about her attitude toward the future. In her 2021 book *Rememberings*, she said this was her first memoir, but it wouldn't be her last. But after her seventeen-year-old son, Shane, died by suicide in 2022, she wrote in various social media posts, including the final one before her death, that life was no longer worth living. She'd loved Shane endlessly, but ultimately couldn't protect him. The loss—this failure—was killing her.

THIRD

In late summer of 2018, I became pregnant again. It happened quickly after the miscarriage and indeed time was dwindling. I'd be thirty-nine soon, and a blood test determined an exceedingly low egg count. The days following those test results were devastating—my doctor said I'd be unlikely to conceive without IVF—and I had a hard time believing this news wasn't some terrible third omen coming to fruition. This occurred the same week Sinéad performed "Nothing Compares 2 U" on Ireland's *Late Late Show*. She'd considered this her last chance for a comeback and was elated by the subsequent rave reviews. I watched Sinéad sing gloriously in her red abaya and hijab as I cried over my own "U," this possibility of a baby I'd never know.

So the white-magical appearance of the plus sign on the stick, just after we were told it wouldn't happen, felt like a last chance for me, too, during my cautiously optimistic first ultrasound. "Hmmm." The sonographer swept the wand around my already-hardened belly. "One, two . . . one, two," she repeated, lilting her voice like this was some goddamn game of peekaboo. "I can't confirm, but this looks like two sacs."

Minutes later, the doctor confirmed: two homes, two inhabitants. My comedian obstetrician offered my eggs their own rave review. "We thought you were running low on eggs. Turns out you were using them all!"

For decades I'd stacked my Jenga blocks to build my life deliberately: finding someone to love, in my husband, Brock, and with the birth of our daughter—our collaborative creation who unlocked years of stifled creativity—discovering my inspiration to write. While preparing to become parents, Brock and I had smugly quipped, "smart people have just one." But after spending two years falling madly in love with our daughter, we remembered: we weren't all that smart. We'd be complete with *just one more*.

The news of twins was not a blessing, but an impossible psychic and financial yoke—we'd planned for two total children, not three. We lived half a day's drive from family with no support system in the college town where, despite teaching at our university for a decade, our instructor positions still deemed us temporary. After the ultrasound, we briefly—deliriously—wondered if we had an option in aborting one of them. The two technical terms for it are almost comfortingly clinical: "selective termination" and "multifetal pregnancy reduction." Sometimes a twin is aborted because one of them has a terminal disease, but in our case, the selection would be random. Whichever fetus was farthest from the cervix would be selected for termination. A doctor would decide—based on the arbitrary placement of cells—which baby would grow to become ours and which wouldn't. In researching these procedures, that was what I couldn't abide: this ironically extreme dearth of choice. So: we'd let whatever gray magic this was play out, damn the costs to our marriage and mental health.

Just thinking about an abortion again, in a completely different context—older and more mature, with a steady marriage and career—brought to the surface more of the repressed questions and guilt. For years after the procedure, I didn't whisper about my abortion, even to my liberal, supportive mother, much less #shoutyourabortion, as the internet impelled women to do in the late 2010s. I noted my own use of terms: no matter the age of gestation, I called it a baby when I'd wanted it, and a fetus when I didn't. *Were* these babies? Which losses counted?

I could read Sinéad differently, too, now. Revisiting her account of her losses allowed me to see I didn't have to parse my own pain. In that 1991 *Spin* interview, she argued strongly for women's control over their bodies, but said that in terms of grief, it doesn't matter whether one has had an abortion or a miscarriage. They both hurt. "I just believe that if a child is meant to be born it will be born." The "Three Babies" she addressed in song were not meant to be born, yet she claimed to know their faces and smells; she "wrapped [their] cold bodies around me." Though they never quite got to be babies, that's what she called them. Her losses didn't require precise framing; her choices didn't preclude suffering. I heard the song now as about not only recovering from loss but learning to name them all without shame.

It was in this spirit that I arrived at my ten-week ultrasound appointment for the twins, still freshly mourning my miscarriage, yet full of hope. Then, my doctor noted one fetus was measuring much smaller. She'd warned us in advance not to start two new college funds. But we'd told family—we'd told ourselves—that we could do this, that this was our plan. "Not a good sign, but let's wait and see." My suddenly earnest OB was no longer cracking jokes.

That twin didn't die. In medical terms, it vanished. That's what they call it, vanishing twin syndrome, when one of a set of multiples dies in utero and disappears or gets reabsorbed into the body. Grief mixed with relief is a horrible, whiplashing cocktail. I called it "grelief," but no one was in the mood to be amused.

Despite recognizing triaphilia is a myth, I never stopped waiting for the third terrible thing to drop, until it did. My follow-up bloodwork two weeks after the official vanishing showed one baby in utero had tested positive for Trisomy 18, a nearly-always fatal genetic disorder in which three cells rather than two attach to chromosome 18, causing major organ and bodily defects: clubbed feet, underdeveloped heads, malformed lungs, large and irreparable holes in their hearts. *Tri*somy. *Three* fucking cells. And the doctors couldn't say for sure which baby carried it. Most likely the one that "vanished," though it could also be both. We'd have to wait till week twenty—eight excruciating weeks—for an amniocentesis to confirm our still-living baby was Trisomy-free. That the baby would actually live.

Now, late into the evening on Mother's Day 2024, and five months after Sinéad's death is deemed "natural," I lie in bed with my two babies, my daughter and my son. This year my son makes me his first card. He draws our family, and though my daughter is tall for her age, and I'm tiny next to their dad, he depicts me as by far the most towering figure. "Because I love you the most," he says, ignoring his sister's protests about the equilateral nature of our love. He counts us out on the page, "One, two, three, four."

My daughter wonders aloud what our family might be like with five, if her brother's twin hadn't vanished. Our beautiful boy Manny, born under the Gemini sign (twins), on Bob Dylan's birthday: Dylan, Sinéad's hero. Our son's middle name: MacGowan, namesake for Pogues frontman Shane MacGowan, with whom my husband shares a Christmas birthday exactly twenty years apart. The same Shane after whom Sinéad named the beautiful boy she lost a year before her own death.

I tell my daughter I think about that baby a lot, and it makes me sad sometimes.

"It's sad," she agrees, "but it was a fetus, not a baby. And maybe it helped make the perfect Manny." I don't recall ever explaining the terminological differences between fetuses and babies, and I'm not ready to tell her now that I'm no longer interested in making those kinds of distinctions. I'll save for later Sinéad's own words that have helped me grieve her, and them. Because hearing her songs, reading her words, I understand that death, like grief, shouldn't be anatomized as "natural" or "unnatural"; it's just death. It's grief. It will be endured, moved through, no matter what names we give it.

I try now not to count omens, or blessings, or to fear a metaphorically unknown future. I know what I've lost—three babies—and through them I've gained these precious two. "One, two . . . one, two." After I tuck them into bed, I roll them over in my mind, recalling the surprising "you" in the very middle of "Three Babies." I'd never pondered these lines discretely, but Sinéad sings that her three losses "have brought you closer to me." It's unclear whether "you" is one of her future children, or even her future self. I know for sure my *you* are these two. The face on them, the smell of them—they will be with us whenever, wherever, we go. Our family has made its circuitous way to four, but so much has gone into making us who we are. So, after everything, who's counting?

Brambles

"Black Boys on Mopeds"

SARAH VIREN

It was Easter Sunday, 1989, when Nicholas Bramble crashed a friend's moped in the Ladbroke Grove neighborhood of West London. Bramble was seventeen, not twenty-one as would later be reported, and less than a mile from his home. The moped was a Honda 80cc and, though the day has been overcast and stormy, it was night, just past 10:30 p.m. Bramble hit a wall first, then a lamppost, and somewhere in all that movement his helmet flew from his head—at least according to police, who were the only witnesses.

Bramble was known as Nicky in the neighborhood, and what his neighbors discovered in the moments after the crash that caused his death were six police vehicles surrounding the crash site. They assumed, given not only the evidence but also years of experience with police in their community, that officers had been chasing Nicky before he died. Some came to believe that police had intentionally rammed Bramble on his bike, causing it to flip. But the police swore first to local journalists and then at an official inquest that they had not been chasing Nicholas Bramble on his moped that night. Someone nearby had reported Bramble driving suspiciously or erratically, they said, and they had merely been looking for him, only to find him moments too late.

The coroner, a man whose official title was "her Majesty's coroner," acknowledged that "an inordinate number of police vehicles" were present at the crash site, but he accepted the police version of events and called the protests that followed Bramble's death the "creation of racial tension by mischievous people." Local newspapers more or less followed suit, reporting, wrongly, in one article that Bramble had stolen the moped and, in another, describing protesters as having "besieged" a police station—even though a judge would later dismiss all charges against arrested protesters and the British government would open yet another investigation into the conduct of its metropolitan police on the day of the protest.

"The police accused him of stealing a bike he had borrowed from a friend and in the ensuing chase he banged into something and died," Sinéad O'Connor later told the London magazine *The Face* in what is the only article I've found of her mentioning Nicky Bramble by name. "Then they say they weren't even involved. I live round here and I can't help but see how badly Black people are treated. Same as America. Treated like pieces of shit."

There was no other Black boy, or man, on a moped, at least as far as I can tell. But cover art for O'Connor's second album, *I Do Not Want What I Haven't Got,* included the photo of another young Black Londoner who died in police custody, Colin Roach, alongside a photo of his parents standing in the rain after his death, his father holding an umbrella over his mother's head, both looking into the middle distance as one does in grief. Roach was twenty-one when he died, shot at a police station. According to police, he shot himself. This was January of 1983, six years before Bramble died, some eight miles away in the East London neighborhood of Hackney. Police interrogated Roach's father,

James, for hours that night before telling him that Roach was dead. Afterward, they ransacked Colin's bedroom, searching without success for ammunition for the gun they swore he had with him when he entered their station alone that night after being dropped off there by a friend—seeking refuge, that friend later said.

The story of Roach's death became a rallying cry in a larger movement protesting police treatment of London's Black residents in the early 1980s. Fundraisers were organized in the Roach family's name, and a poem written and a film made about Roach's death, both of which asked the same question: "Who killed Colin Roach?" In 1989, the year Bramble died, a group called the Roach Family Support Committee published a book-length report on Roach's death, raising substantial and lasting questions about the police version of events.

Perhaps because of the comparable attention paid to Colin's story, when writers and journalists have, in the years since, gotten the facts wrong about the story behind O'Connor's song "Black Boys on Mopeds," the most common mistake I've seen is to conflate Bramble's life and death with Roach's. There is, for instance, a 2020 article in the *Durango Herald* declaring "Black Boys on Mopeds" the greatest protest song of all time, then narrating a story in which Colin Roach, not Nicky Bramble, is on a moped that night, "when police give chase, assuming he must have stolen it." There is, too, the website, "Two Story Melody," dedicated to telling the story behind various songs, and in its telling of "Black Boys on Mopeds," Nicky Bramble is again absent and Colin Roach is on the moped when police show up: "Muddied actions ensue and Roach ends up in the foyer of a police station, quickly expiring from a gunshot wound."

Even Sinéad O'Connor bungled the story a bit, decades later—her memory sapped, she explains near the end of her memoir, by depression and treatment for that disease. Despite the story she'd told a London journalist about Nicky Bramble in 1990, and despite subsequent stories about that story around the same time, she writes in her memoir that the song was inspired by *two* teenagers in her London neighborhood who "had taken a cousin's moped without asking permission; the cops were called and gave chase, the boys got frightened, crashed, and died." It is a version of reality that hews more closely to the lyrics of the song itself, and perhaps because of that fact, along with the seemingly reliable provenance, this version was also repeated in a *Guardian* article about O'Connor's top ten songs, which was published shortly after her death in 2023.

I'm not sure why the elisions or mistakes in articles about "Black Boys on Mopeds" bother me. The song is still a protest song, no matter the facts or inventions buried within the stories we tell about it. It still unleashes a force both unfurling and wild in me when I hear it, and still speaks to larger social ills—both institutional racism and the government's refusal to address that racism. And the song has always been about more than its title or refrain. There is the hypocrisy of Margaret Thatcher after the massacre in Tiananmen Square. There is a mother of three begging for food at Smithfield. And there is Sinéad O'Connor herself, singing about trying to save her new baby boy from the griefs of this world.

But the power of the song, for me, has always been in the refrain: what England isn't and what it is. I listened to "Black Boys on Mopeds" for the first time in the early 1990s, a teenager, coming to terms with my own loss of faith in my country, one I had been raised to believe was, if not a mythical land, then at least a good one. It was 2023, the day O'Connor died, when I began listening to "Black Boys on Mopeds" again on repeat, just as I once had when I was young, only now I am also a mother, well versed in the desire for a world in which to raise my kids, all kids, without any sense of grieving. The following year, around Easter, still listening to that song on repeat, I began trying to track down the story behind it. I knew my search wouldn't change anything about the song itself. Songs are not replicas of reality—nor should they be. But I wanted to better understand the story that inspired O'Connor to write it, as well as the context within which she wrote it. It became important to know, as best I could, what was and what wasn't true about that story.

In an online archive of British newspapers, I found four articles written about Bramble's death in spring of 1989, and then dozens more that mention him once O'Connor's song came out the following year. But all the stories were barebone. Nicholas Bramble was seventeen. He died in the hospital. Ten people were arrested in the subsequent protests. One or two mentioned where he lived before he died, and I mapped that area of London, found what it looks like now, and, eventually, on Facebook, found several groups dedicated to remembering the history of the neighborhoods Nicky Bramble once called home: Ladbroke Grove and North Kensington, but also Notting Hill. In two groups, no one had heard of him, but in the third, my post about Nicky quickly received more than a dozen comments.

"I was in Oxford Gardens children's home at the time, we were the same age," one woman responded. "From what I remember the police chased him on the bike and knocked him off, causing his death. Nicky was cool."

"I remember this so well," another wrote. "I was young and from what I recall the police had thought it was my cousin riding the bike. They went to my auntie's house to tell her that my cousin had been killed in an accident on his moped. Sadly, they went to identify the body and it turned out that it wasn't my cousin but Nicky."

Neither of those women "walked to talk," but around that same time I found mention of a 2022 book that tells the story of the mostly Caribbean and African community in the neighborhood where Bramble grew up. *The Frontline: The Story of Struggle, Resistance and Black Identity in Notting Hill* is hard to find in print, but its editor, Ishmahil Blagrove Jr., emailed me several quotes from testimonies included in the book. He said he remembered both Bramble's death and the protests that followed, but he also knew of many other stories about police violence in the neighborhood—including one of his own.

"I share these testimonies to give you an idea of the cat and mouse atmosphere that Nicky would have had to navigate daily," he wrote, before mentioning one concern he had about my interest in tracking down the facts of this story now. "(A)sking questions about Nicky's death, 35 years later, solely in regards to lyrics of a Sinéad O'Connor song," he wrote, "is a little discomforting. Nevertheless, I hope something positive and meaningful for Nicky will come out of your research." I wrote back that I hoped it would, too—and said that I agreed: someone should have written a more complete story about Nicky's life and death when he died, not now, and not because of a song.

"Black Boys on Mopeds" is one of O'Connor's most requested songs, one that's been covered by artists from Sharon Van Etten and Shea Rose to the metal band Chevelle and is often cited in stories proclaiming, as *The Nation* did recently, that "Sinéad O'Connor Always Knew That Black Lives Matter." And yet when it was released, the song, like the album itself, was not met with immediate acclaim.

"With her gently dramatic version of the Prince song 'Nothing Compares 2 U' still deservedly notched at the top of the best-sellers," the *Guardian* rock critic Robin Denselow wrote in March of 1990,

"Sinéad O'Connor follows up with a typically infuriating album that shows off both her considerable strengths and her lack of judgement." Those strengths, he continued, show when O'Connor is "at her most personal, dealing with topics like fame, pregnancy, babies or religion" while her alleged immaturity can be found in songs such as "Black Boys on Mopeds," which Denselow called "another embarrassment, a bizarre outburst that equates Mrs. Thatcher with massacres in China."

Other critics that year characterized the song as an "anti-Thatcher diatribe," an "angry, anti-government song," a "gratuitous piece of England-bashing," and "aggressively provocative." Don McLeese, writing for the *Chicago Sun-Times*, admitted liking it, but, echoing many critics at the time, he also accused O'Connor of naïveté. "If she really believes she can find a home where her son won't be aware that there's any such thing as grieving," he wrote, "I'd love to reserve a plot in the same Fantasyland."

Sinéad O'Connor was a new mother when she wrote "Black Boys on Mopeds," her oldest son Jake close to a year old. She lived in Ladbroke Grove, Bramble's neighborhood, and likely heard about his death not, as some journalists later claimed, from the spare coverage of it in the mainstream press, but from her neighbors and friends. Jebb Johnson, who formed part of the neighborhood line of defense that Blagrove writes about in his book, told me he remembered O'Connor hanging out at a local record store during those years. Her manager was well connected in the community, he said, and she was friends with a local activist and musician named DJ Lepke, formally Leroy Anderson, who started Dread Broadcasting Corporation, England's first pirate radio station dedicated to reggae, soul, and funk.

"We had a lot of respect for her," Johnson said. "She was held in high esteem locally—and not everyone was."

Which is not to say that Sinéad O'Connor is a hero in this story. She was only one voice—and she sometimes got it wrong. In one interview, after the album's release, for instance, she joked that the Black boys on mopeds were men she'd like to date. But even if she later forgot or fudged the specifics, O'Connor knew Bramble's story well when she wrote that song, and she centered his death, along with Colin Roach's, because she thought the rest of the world needed to know those stories, too.

As Blagrove pointed out in our emails back and forth, however, to know only Bramble's story, or only Roach's for that matter, would also be to err in telling the larger story of this one song. His book, *The Frontline*, is about the harassment and abuse faced by Black Londoners in Bramble's community, but also about those who formed a frontline of support to protect Black businesses and residents. The nucleus of that movement was a civil rights leader named Frank Crichlow, who owned a restaurant and gathering spot called The Mangrove that was raided by police at least a dozen times in the late '60s and early '70s. Crichlow, who died in 2010, was one of nine arrested in 1970 on false charges of inciting a riot, a story chronicled in Steve McQueen's 2020 historical drama *Mangrove*. Crichlow was cleared of those charges, but arrested again, this time on drug charges, in 1988, and cleared of those in a jury trial the following year, two months after Bramble's death. His lawyers argued at the time that police had conspired to plant drugs on Crichlow as a way of shutting down the line of defense he and others like Jebb Johnson had up until then maintained.

"They don't like people who stand up for their rights," Crichlow told a local reporter after the jury found him not guilty on all counts.

There was no such tale of atonement in either Roach's or Bramble's cases. According to the official record, both still died either by accident or suicide, and the police had no role in their deaths. But that's not the version you see if you search for Nicky Bramble now, and in that way,

I suppose, all the mistakes add up to one larger truth. The articles that do mention Nicky all say he was being chased by police. They all implicate the police in his death—the official record be damned.

I thought about that shift in what is known or believed when I came back to "Black Boys on Mopeds" recently, only somewhat more enlightened about who Nicky Bramble was and how he died on Easter of 1989. There is a conversation throughout that song that O'Connor seems to be having with someone: her son, her community, her critics, all of us. She admits this person might think her childish, presumably for both her anger and her idealism, but she reminds them, reminds us, that if the world hates her, it will also hate you. Which is to say, I think, that we cannot disengage ourselves, disconnect our interlocking lives, from grief or hate, but also that sometimes you have to stand apart to more clearly see what it is, and what it isn't.

"Remember what I told you," O'Connor sings, and listening, I hope we will.

Girl You Better Try to Have Fun

"Nothing Compares 2 U"

MEGAN STIELSTRA

That summer in Alaska, I cried at everything. Of course I did. My dad was dying, but I was refusing to accept that fact so instead I cried watching the sunrise over the ocean. I cried watching whales breach off the side of the boat. I cried watching him gut fish with my teenage son, the ooze and blood and final flutter. I cried because Marilyn introduced me as her daughter and her kids introduced me as their sister and nobody used the word *step*. I cried because my sixteen-year-old niece asked if we could listen to "Wannabe" in the car. I cried because my two-year-old niece had on llama pajamas and they were too awesome to handle. I cried because I wanted salad and the produce shipment from the mainland hadn't come in yet. I cried when Rob got off the plane and my dad came out to the tarmac to greet him.

They hadn't seen each other for thirty years, not since Rob and I dated in high school. We broke up a few weeks before the senior prom and I will never forget the look on my dad's face as he watched my first gut-punch heartbreak: sitting on the dock in our backyard in Michigan, our feet in the lake, me crying my face off, him saying it would all be okay. "The sun will come up," he told me. "I promise you, it's coming."

I was sixteen then, and my dad was almost fifty, the same age I am now, and I understand more about heartbreak. The gut-punch, sure, but also what comes after.

A year before that summer in Alaska, I was visiting my mother in my hometown back in Michigan, still raw from my recent divorce, and I ran into Rob again. I mean this literally: I was out for a run along the Huron River, I rounded a bend, and there he was. We stopped. The wind stopped. I could hear my own heartbeat. At work I'd been editing a book about eternalism, the philosophical theory that the past, present, and future are all happening simultaneously, and it felt like proof. I was forty-six. I was sixteen. I was sixty, seventy, eighty, looking back down the line of my life to that moment by the river when everything made sense.

The airport was at the far end of the island. Around us were mountains, a planet of sky. So many miles to get here. So many decades. "Glad you finally decided to join the family," my dad said to Rob on the tarmac. They both cried. I was already crying. I'd been crying for days.

Honestly?—it was perfect.

We were all still here.

"Sinéad O'Connor died," my sister called from the living room and snap your fingers—that's how fast I started sobbing. It was the end of July—July 26, 2023, to be precise—and I was in the kitchen making coffee. Kim and I worked remotely that summer, logging on to Zoom every morning at five a.m. to show up in Eastern time zones. The rest of the house was asleep: my kid, her kids, our brothers and their kids, Marilyn, Rob—everyone except my dad. He was already out on the ocean. He liked to watch the sunrise. "It always comes up," he'd say: when I cried on the dock after the prom, when he and my mom split up, when I told him my husband left me, when he told me he had cancer. "I know it's dark right now," he said. "But the sun will come up. I promise you, it's coming."

"Are you okay?" Kim asked, coming into the kitchen. I wasn't, of course. I was a fucking mess. I didn't have language then to explain but I've got it now: that summer in Alaska, I was remembering how to feel. At some point in the preceding years—the pandemic, the divorce, trying to find work, living in four different states alone with a twelve-year-old, isolated from every support system in a country submerged in collective grief—I'd hit an internal switch, pulled the *off* lever on my insides. "Vampires turn their feelings on and off," my son told me once. He liked horror. He liked sci-fi. "They don't want to feel pain so they stop feeling anything at all."

"What happens when they start again?" I asked.

"They feel everything."

Kim was visibly alarmed. My face was a faucet. I gasped and choked and leaked into the coffee. "I'm so sorry," she said, wrapping around me like a vine. "You must have really loved her music."

Love is the wrong word in the context of Sinéad O'Connor. Let's try *live.* I lived her music; the soundtrack to my life. I see many of you nodding in agreement, us feral women of the nineties, our memories choreographed to her velvet razor of a voice. The morning of my divorce, I turned up the volume on "The Last Day of Our Acquaintance" and scream-sang along, knowing that decades of almost ex-wives had felt this same release. When I was pregnant and scared I'd never write again, I remembered that she recorded *The Lion and the Cobra* in her last trimester and knew I was joining a thriving coven of ferocious mother-artists. The lyrics from "I Do Not Want What I Haven't Got" replaced the Bene Gesserit Litany Against Fear as my secret teenage mantra for how to keep going in this mess of a world; to this day I repeat them, under my breath, over and over until my pulse slows, until my rage feels rational.

Her songs have shaped me.

Especially—Well. You know the one.

Try not to sing along when it comes on the radio. Try not to stretch the word *wrong* into four syllables, the *want* into five. Try not to time travel, back to your years-ago aching self, or maybe the ache is right now. Loss comes for all of us, at any age—a parent, a partner, a dream.

The statistics are legend: "Nothing Compares 2 U" charted at number one in seventeen countries. It won Video of the Year at the 1990 MTV Music Video Awards. It was the #1 World Single at the first Billboard Music Awards, topping the Billboard Hot 100 for four straight weeks. This acclaim meant nothing to me at fifteen; I just wanted her voice. I remember waiting impatiently for Casey Kasem to count down the American Top 40 so I could record it on my boom box and rewind 'til the tape snagged. Here's what I heard when Sinéad sang: *girls can feel*. It felt shocking—subversive, even—for a woman to be loud, wrecked, angry, honest. I lived in small-town Southeast Michigan, Midwest nice. I'd never seen emotion like that, let alone heard it. It would be a couple more years before I understood what she was singing about, standing at the prom in my pretty dress, my fishnet tights, watching Rob dance with another girl. It had been two weeks—"seven hours and fifteen days"—and there he was with his arms around someone else.

The opening strings filled our high school gym.

I let myself feel it.

"Good morning," Rob said as he walked into the kitchen, and then: "Oh. Hey. Come here." I felt myself moved from Kim's hug into his. There's something about arriving at a place of safety that lets us lose it completely and never in my life have I lost it so completely. I cried because Sinéad O'Connor was dead. I cried because Joan Didion was dead, and Tina Turner, and all the artists I hadn't grieved because apparently I was a vampire and somewhere in 2020 I'd turned myself off and now that I was on again I couldn't stop. bell hooks was dead. Milan Kundera was dead. Valerie Boyd was dead. Don't tell me it's silly to mourn people we don't know personally—those artists let me feel. They help me access my own heart. They keep me from remaining numb, complacent, complicit. What's the line?—*between grief and nothing*? I've done the nothing. I've done the numb, the careless, the empty, and I'll tell you what: I'm with Faulkner. I choose life. I choose living. I choose feeling, even when it hurts. My dad was dying and it hurt.

He was dying. He was dying. He was dying.

Music lives in the body. I hear the opening strings and I'm back in my high school gym. To carry an artist in your bones across decades is miraculous enough, but Sinéad O'Connor took it even further; her influence on me and so many of us spanned far beyond the visceral, sense-memory response. She got in our *brains*.

Do you remember?—in 1991 "Nothing Compares 2 U" was nominated for three Grammys and she declined to show up, criticizing the music industry in an open letter and subsequent interviews for honoring material gain as opposed to artistic merit. "How can we communicate with and help the human race," she wrote, "when we have allowed ourselves to be taken out of the world and placed above it?" I can't overstate what a vital lesson that was for a teenage girl—hell, for any of us, wherever we're at on the line of our life. It was the first time I remember a woman saying no. It made me ask why she said no, and the search for that why showed me that a song is so much more than a song, that music and language are tools. We can make this world better. We can *make* things. With the aid of a very dedicated librarian (I love you, librarians), I read into the politics of her music, what it means to stand for something as an artist and a human being. It helped me differentiate between the making of art and the selling of art, a lesson I carry to this day in my tangled jobs as both a writer and a publisher.

She also got me thinking about different perspectives and ways of seeing through the seemingly simple act of covering a song. You can't talk about "Nothing Compares 2 U" without talking about Prince, who wrote and first recorded the song in 1985 with his funk-pop band, The Family. He never spoke publicly about what inspired the lyrics, though it was speculated to be about the loss of his longtime housekeeper Sandy Scipioni. I was shocked to hear O'Connor say, in the 2022 documentary *Nothing Compares*, that for her, the song was about the death of her mother. For me at fifteen—and again at forty-five, when my marriage imploded—it was about the loss of romantic love. Shortly after my husband left, a friend sent me Aretha Franklin's jazzy 2014 cover, and I had a sort of epiphany (there was bourbon involved) around the lyric "Girl you better try to have fun." In the O'Connor version, that line was all rage, some jackass fool belittling the depth of her pain. But in the Franklin version, the line gave me a choice. *I know it hurts,* she seemed to be saying. *But baby—you're alive. Go out there and try to have fun!*

Believe you me: I did.

At some point I cried myself out. Kim made a fresh pot of coffee. Rob suggested we go to Safeway; Marilyn told him they were expecting a produce shipment and he knew I wanted salad. He couldn't deliver me from the heartbreak, but lettuce—lettuce was a thing he could do. He piled bags of it into the cart while I wandered around in a post-cry hangover, when all the endorphins have poured out your nose and everything feels slow-motion. That's when I heard it: through the grocery store's stereo system, the opening strings.

It was still early in Alaska. The radio was waking up to what the internet already knew.

I looked at Rob, wondering if he remembered. It was so long ago, back down the line of my life. He held out his hand. "You know," he said, pulling me in for a dance. Above our heads, the word *want* had five syllables. "If memory serves, I owe you a prom."

Back at the house, we ran into my dad in the driveway, fresh from the boat with a cooler full of gutted salmon. He was months into chemo but hadn't slowed down; fishing every morning, hiking with his dogs, playing with his grandkids, telling his daughter it would all be okay.

"Hey," he said as I passed him on the steps. He put a hand on my cheek and tilted my face, red and puffy from crying. "You okay, kid?"

He always called me kid. I was forty-eight, I was sixteen, I was six, seven, eight. "Well," I said. There were so many things I wanted to say in the moment but I didn't know the right words. "Sinéad O'Connor died," I said instead.

"I'm so sorry," he said. "Was she a friend of yours?"

I laughed. It felt good to laugh. "Something like that," I said.

Six months later I would go back to the island and spend his last few weeks with him, the gift of my life. I got to say what I wanted to say. I figured out the words. We will always figure out the words. We open our mouths or we pick up a pen and we try.

"Have fun," he said on the steps.

I thought he was talking about the rest of the day. "I will," I said.

"I mean it," he said. I looked at his face and my own looked back. "I want you to have fun."

A Mother-Daughter Blood Story

"Jump in the River"

MAY-LEE CHAI

When I first heard "Jump in the River" in 1990, I was twenty-three and I'd just returned to the U.S. after studying and working in China. I'd been living in my father's erstwhile hometown of Nanjing during the year of martial law imposed after the government's violent crackdown on student demonstrators at Tiananmen Square. Everything from mail to radio broadcasts had been curtailed, so I hadn't been able to listen to new music.

I'd been looking for a place to call home, and while I had enjoyed living in Nanjing where I could reasonably blend in, so long as I didn't open my mouth, where I didn't have to experience anti-Chinese racism, living under an authoritarian regime was difficult, so I returned to the U.S., still looking for that safe harbor.

Then I discovered Sinéad O'Connor. Finally, a voice that expressed what I felt inside. All these turbulent emotions that I could not yet put words to, she was able to vocalize. I loved how Sinéad snarled and howled, hit the high notes like she was throwing a bomb and scraped the low like a caged tiger growling through the iron bars. I didn't have a lot of money, but after I was hired to work as a reporter in Denver, I was able to purchase cassettes of albums one and two, *The Lion and the Cobra* and *I Do Not Want What I Haven't Got*.

My mother, however, hated Sinéad.

"Why is she always screaming?" my mother complained, making me immediately feel like screaming myself.

I don't know why I had tried to play Sinéad's music for my mother. Perhaps I'd imagined that it would be a way for me to connect with my mother's pride in her maternal Irish roots.

My mother and I had very different tastes in music. When I was growing up, I had not been allowed to listen to most kinds of music. My father, who was Chinese, had PTSD from having grown up as a child of war in China during the Sino-Japanese War. From the ages of nine to thirteen, he'd had to hide in air-raid shelter caves as Japanese bombers strafed the city of Chongqing, where his family had taken refuge. The sound of drums drove him into a rage. He'd scream, smash things, call us names. No rock and roll or even classical music was allowed.

My mother, who was white, liked to listen to religious music. Not soul or gospel but tapes of an elderly Catholic nun called Mother Angelica who could not carry a tune. I felt trapped in the car with my mother as we drove across the country—my mother was afraid of flying—to visit my grandmother while Sister's cassettes droned on for the ten-and-a-half-hour journey.

Finding music that I liked was new to me, a once-forbidden fruit.

But now when my mother visited me, she complained about Sinéad. She didn't want to hear her cassette while I drove her around Denver. She didn't want to hear the cassette I had in my boom box on the floor of my apartment.

The more my mother complained, the more I needed to listen to Sinéad, putting us into a dead-end loop of conflict.

My mother hadn't liked the fact that I'd gone to study in China.

"You're siding with him," she'd wailed. By *him* she meant my father. "But you're half me," she said. "You're half my daughter, too."

"I have a right to be proud of my Chinese heritage," I said. "I am your daughter, but people see me as Asian and I need knowledge to protect myself."

My mother didn't respond. She looked away, annoyed, angry that I was talking back, perhaps. As a child, I was not allowed to "talk back" to my parents, to adults. I was told that in order to be a good child, thus a desired and loved child, I had to hold my tongue, no matter what terrible, cruel things adults might say to and about me. This was the hierarchy of the world, and it had been beaten into my mother's body by her own parents.

I didn't like the idea that my mother thought studying Chinese was picking a side. Or the idea that I was only half her daughter. Wasn't everyone who was biologically descended from their parents only half each parent's DNA? Unless you were cloned, I suppose. But who else said their child was only half theirs? My father didn't.

It hurt me when my mother talked this way.

I had nowhere to put my emotions, now that I had nowhere on earth to run away to, but when I listened to "Jump in the River" it was like the universe had sent me a personal gift. I put the track on endless repeat in my Walkman as I jogged, mile after mile, trying to escape my own emotions, the infectious danceable beat contrasting with the violence of the lyrics, sex and blood commingling: "Like the times we did it so hard/there was blood on the wall."

This was how I felt when my mother complained, when she cried and said I was hurting her, when she called me half a daughter, claimed I was picking sides.

Blood on the wall indeed.

The song ostensibly is sexual, about lovers, but like so much of

Sinéad's music, it could also be about mothers, daughters, abuse, our love that hurts yet persists. Our mothers who bleed to give birth to us then return the favor by extracting blood with their words (if we're lucky) or more (if we're not). This is how I came to the song, as a balm and a record of mother love and hate, of my emotions which I could not name, did not know how to name, could barely endure feeling.

Looking back, I ask my younger self: Why did it matter if my mother liked the musician I loved? Why had I tried to share Sinéad's music in the first place? But I was a young woman, and I still needed my mother. I wanted my mother's love. I couldn't understand why she didn't love Sinéad the way I did.

And I thought I could reach her still, my mother.

Hadn't she dared to give birth to me despite all the naysayers and racists who'd tried to stop her? When my parents married in 1966, it was still a year before the landmark Supreme Court case *Loving* v. *Virginia* would strike down all the anti-miscegenation laws across the U.S. My parents had told me what people had said to them after they announced their engagement. The president of the university where my father worked, my mother's coworkers, the former missionaries down the street, the nurse in the hospital: *But surely you won't have children?* And my mother, herself a young woman, retorted, "Of course we're going to have children!" Wasn't that the reason she'd accepted my father's marriage proposal? Because he said he'd wanted to have children, to start a family, while her longtime (white) boyfriend had always complained, "I don't think it's fair to bring children into this world," despite his life of privilege, his trust fund cushion.

And weren't we a happy family once? Aren't there the pictures to prove it? The outings to the beach, to the mountains, to Chinese restaurants on Sundays with my father's family? We're laughing, smiling, happy to be together. I remember.

It was only later, when I was twelve and we moved to a rural community in South Dakota, that we had to face nonstop racist hatred. White people in that small town called my father, brother, and me racist slurs to our faces. White men drove by our house shooting. Five of our dogs were shot dead and left for us to find at the end of the driveway over the years. Racists sent hate mail; I remember the letter addressed in block writing to "The Chinaman and the Floozy."

And my mother, overwhelmed, grew silent. When white people told a racist joke in front of her, about me, about my brother, I watched her smile and say nothing. When white kids called us names in school, she told us to laugh along, "Show them you can take a joke." But I didn't think their slurs were funny. When white veterans told me about sex workers they'd visited in tours of duty in Asia, I tried to talk with her about my discomfort and she reacted with jealousy that I'd attracted male attention. I wanted her to protect me, but instead I felt even dirtier.

When I tried to talk to my mother about the racism we were experiencing as a family, she would leave the room, or else grow angry . . . at me. "Sourpuss!" she called me. "Why can't you be happy? You were a happy baby. I remember!"

I thought about killing myself. If my mother didn't love me, what point was there in being alive?

This feeling is what I recalled when Sinéad, overcome by the intensity of her emotions, sings that she'd jump in the river if her beloved told her to. *Wouldn't it be a good idea to jump?* I thought. Whether to douse myself in cold water, substituting a physical sensation for an emotional one, or to drown, to cease feeling at all.

When I left for college, I vowed to find a way. To find a safe place for myself. And I hoped I'd find a way to bring my mother back from the dissociative well into which she'd fallen.

I knew she came from an abusive family, a violent alcoholic father who beat her mother even when she was pregnant, a mother who took out her anguish on the body of her eldest daughter, that is, my mother. I knew Mama had grown up in a time and place when it was legal for a man to beat his wife and children, when the police did not have to respond to domestic violence. Grandma had told me how Gramps would get in fights with other men in bars, but when the sheriff's deputies brought him home, they admonished her, not him: "You need to keep a better eye on your husband!"

I knew about the time Gramps punched my mother in the face and knocked out her tooth for refusing to eat the pet rabbits he'd cooked. She was seventeen. The time he punched her for opening the oven and causing a cake to fall. She was nine. The time Grandma beat her with a switch until she bled because she'd invited a Black neighbor over to the house for pie. She was six.

I knew why my mother was silenced.

But I also knew the mother who'd believed so fervently in love that she'd married my father and given birth to me (*Twenty hours of labor!*) and my brother (*Only a year later*). I remembered how she'd shared her favorite books with me when I was growing up (*I always loved to read*), and how she'd consoled me after I flunked the Presidential Fitness Test yet again (*I never liked P.E., either*).

So I continued to listen to Sinéad, her music giving me the release I needed, while I searched for the words to explain my feelings to my mother.

Then finally, a breakthrough.

I was in graduate school at CU-Boulder, and my mother was visiting.

My mother was in bed watching television in the front room, while I worked on my Chinese homework at my wicker table in the kitchenette, listening to Sinéad on my Walkman so Mama wouldn't hear and complain.

Next up, it's Sinéad O'Connor, an announcer's voice said. I ran out, sliding onto the floor next to the futon I'd rolled out for my mother, just in time for Sinéad's performance on *Saturday Night Live*. We watched together as she delivered a grim, a cappella version of Bob Marley's "War" and then paused, unsmiling, before presenting a picture of the pope to the camera, tearing it up, and proclaiming, "Fight the real enemy."

I heard my mother beside me exhale. "That's the best thing that bald Sinéad has ever done!" she exclaimed. My mother was the eldest of eight, parentified child, second mother to her siblings, dutiful daughter to her mother, her poor mother. (*Mother always looked so womanly, I always felt so thin in comparison*, Mama used to say to me. *I didn't realize it was because she was always pregnant*.) My mother clapped her hands. Then she laughed. A bright chortle from deep within her chest. "That Pope is always speaking out against birth control," Mama said, shaking her head.

She picked up the phone on the end table by her futon and called one of her friends, an Irish woman from her prayer group. "You won't believe what that bald Sinéad has done, Imelda. It's wonderful!" she proclaimed.

The next day, she allowed me to play "Jump in the River" as I drove her around Boulder in my car. In fact, Mama never argued with me about Sinéad again.

Our own personal miracle.

As You Summon Steel

"The Last Day of Our Acquaintance"

SONYA HUBER

In my sad and wistful college days in Minnesota, the dorm room smelled like cinder blocks, linoleum, dust, and a hint of spilled beer. I tucked the cassette of *I Do Not Want What I Haven't Got* into the wooden crate that once held glass bottles of Coca-Cola and slid it under my bed. We had seen and heard Sinéad, her voice a whisper to a snarl, and we were all shaving our heads. The bomb of gender seemed to explode around us as we protested the bombs our country was raining down on Iraq. We were all so angry then and so lit with the joy of finding that anger. Sinéad was not alone in that; we wanted to stop the train of death and she gave it voice.

I had fallen into a depression, left school, kissed a girl, and had my own long brown hair zipped off. The wind on my scalp gave me some clarity. Because my eyes looked larger without the curtain of my hair, I felt I could finally see, as though I could face the world as a person and enjoy a reprieve from the hey-baby and why-don't-you-smile and the long list of other expectations associated with my gender. I told my boyfriend—the Westchester granola boy I'd met at an antiwar protest in Minneapolis—that I kissed a girl.

He shaved off his own long dark locks and broke up with me. We were each other's first college relationship, had been together for over a year, yet both of us were still hung up on our high school sweethearts and thought that every love would feel like first love if we tried hard enough. We didn't even have enough in common to want a friendship after it was done. "The Last Day of Our Acquaintance" was spooled and flipped over and over in my tape player, the sweet and sad thread of her voice with the bare hint of a strumming guitar.

Freshly single, I threw myself into something that could wash over me. Radio and video were like a river then, a bright flashing current that you could wait near and hit record at the perfect moment. And how could you not fall in love with her, this fierce warrior with the diadem of her shorn head, so much more magnetic than the boyfriend I'd just lost, whose sharp voice seemed to promise a blade to cut through the cotton batting of my brain's fog and the muddiness of my future? Catching her songs in a shop or on the airwaves stopped us completely, and we stepped into her voice as the song attached to the moment when it lived in the air.

I carried the idea of love as a still-innocent girl might have heard it, the sense that love just happened to you like the weather, that little could be done to choose its shape or outcome. I'd wanted to talk more with my high school boyfriend; I'd been scared of my hippie college boyfriend's moods; I'd shared the kiss and more with the woman from the coffee shop where we worked, but that felt so positive and easy that I was confused, thinking the lack of drama meant lack of passion. I dealt these three loves over and over like cards in a limited tarot deck, thinking this was the range of love. The common denominator seemed to be that I wanted the wrong things, that love would be easier if I wanted less. I imagined the ending of every love might feel the same, a concentration of sweet memories grown heady and fermented with age to sip in a heart-rent swoon.

When Sinéad sang about meeting in "somebody's office," I was awed by the steel it would take to have the dream of a marriage die, to have to pay someone to help you kill it. I was still holding the hope that a real adult love was out there, hovering and approaching, that would feel solid and transformative and real. Beneath that wish were hard nuggets of specific hurt, dreams that turned to disappointment, which made my wishes more urgent.

When Sinéad prepared John Reynolds, her partner in music and the father of her child, to hear the song for the first time in the Chastain Park studios in Atlanta, she said, "Come in and get loud and come out when I nod my head," he writes. He played the drums following her lead, and "after the first run-through we decided it was as close to perfection as it could ever be." She wrote the song and played it for him, and in the fooling around and jamming the perfect, perfect version was born between them of her brilliance.

She had loved John, began dating him in 1985 as he recorded and produced her songs and played drums to support her iconic voice. They had a baby, Jake, when she was twenty, all the swirling of global superstardom coming for her a few months later with the release of *The Lion and the Cobra*. She had an abortion later that year and married John in 1989, but the song and the living of it was finished by September 1990, when she performed it on *Saturday Night Live*. In those years, she had also been having an affair with her manager, Fachtna Ó Ceallaigh, which ended, and *Rolling Stone* describes the song as the dissolution of "a business arrangement and a love affair." But Fachtna would remain her manager until 2012, with a court battle lasting until 2019. Some day in 1990 was when her experience turned into the imagined last day of the song.

The song had separated from her life into its own story and its own existence, and we'll never know how personal it was, if she felt taken for granted, if Fachtna stopped holding her hand when planes took off, what prompted the rupture. The meeting in someone's office with John to begin the divorce must have happened in 1991, but their acquaintance and artistic partnership lasted through decades as he produced six of her albums and toured with her in 2013. He would fly to Chicago in 2019 during a crisis to bring her home to Ireland. I am so glad she had that.

Hearing Sinéad's voice for the first time created the feeling of having always known it—having lived the space exactly where this deep wave needed to crash. And a girl knows despite her hope that marriage is business, that the teeth of the law and the danger of a planted seed meant a baby and what it might do to a world. We all knew this. The song sparked dread and denial, sympathy with a heartbroken woman and hoping to hell it would not be me.

Even now, I have a slight internal wince every time she sings the word "the seed," and maybe I'm imagining it but it feels like her tongue and throat pull back from giving the word its full force, as if she had to sing around something stuck in her throat. Maybe it was the seed of dissolution, a betrayal, or a mistake? The seed of doubt? No, we knew, because she told us: exactly when you're pregnant with someone's child was when things shifted. It was always stressed that to a fertile field, seeds meant love and danger. She told us, gently and firmly at first, that this would happen. We knew this was coming; somehow I also knew this was coming for me.

And I chose badly, or I chose who seemed right at the time and I invested him with all my hope, and it was a far worse choice than Sinéad made. She would have more marriages and always heartbreak. We blame ourselves: "I've got a bad picker." Even the meanness of others is our fault.

There is a particular loneliness in being pregnant, protecting a life, and knowing you are not protected, are not seen, are talking but are not listened to anymore. And then you must make yourself into a mother and a motherfucker. You learn to be soft as you summon steel; you knit this steel out of air. You have got to make some decisions, and your hopes about whether a man will rally to the cause of new life feel like cinders, and you carry them, blow on them to rouse flame, even as they burn you. You are going to carry them for a few more years, cinders in one hand, baby in the other.

It's astounding to me now that only ten years had passed between my high school breakup and meeting the man I would marry. In those ten years I waited for a signal to cut through my confusion, a clear sign of love that would last. So I chose the man who seemed to want me the most, who barraged me with notes and flowers and paintings, who told me stories of wreckage and pain, because his wanting felt like love. His wanting, his need, his voracious appetite for substances and me and for things to be easier in his life became the dramatic weather of my days, an extended crisis with clear signals and commands, until I felt devoured.

Eventually I figured out, with help, that love did not have to be like this. When I was steeling myself through years of wanting to leave with a young child, I repeated this phrase: "a pound of flesh." I knew he would extract this from me because I knew his ways; I saw them every day. I knew I needed to be ready to run through a rain of crashing agony, that something would be taken from me in the process, something of my body, of my flesh, that it would shred my nervous system, but that I would take the impact, not my child.

But first, we met in so many people's offices: counselors, mostly, and I waited for him to bring up his issues with the first one and of course he didn't and I was too afraid because the baby was small and I was not sleeping and how could this be my life. By the second time, years later in another state, in a small Georgia town that smelled of pine and baked clay where I was teaching, I had a better paycheck coming in and I was ready. My anger had been banked. As Sinéad's lines repeat, "You used to hold my hand when the plane took off," they buzz with a sort of swing on the words *plane* and *somebody's office,* a sense of stepping back to enjoy the words as words. This is the sign of having forged a second self.

I borrowed back the five hundred dollars I'd loaned a friend for her divorce from a man who pointed a gun at her, and I used that five hundred dollars as a down payment on mine. I found the cheapest lawyer to start the divorce but then moved on to another lawyer as things got complicated and chaotic. We never met in somebody's office for the divorce because I had 911 on my list of contacts after he left me such threatening voicemails that I became scared for my life.

I went alone to another office, through a buzzed security door into a cinder block domestic violence shelter where I was counseled on how to make emergency plans. The label "DV" was added in a bright sticker to other folders bearing my name, sorting us based on his danger. The man I'd begun to date met me on campus beneath a magnolia tree in the sun, and I sat down in the grass and said, "I thought I was smart," damning myself for someone else's touch of evil. "He never hit me" is a phrase we used to say, once upon a time, to draw a line between physical and emotional/verbal abuse. May that line rest in the dirt. May it never confuse another generation.

And I was a queen of finalizing the details, a warrior. I compiled a thick binder of notes and photos and voicemail transcripts that caused a judge in a small town in rural Georgia to say to him, "You should never treat the mother of your child this way." I'm sure he doesn't remember any of this happening, as he was usually high. He was full of scorn and victimized innocence for what I was making him suffer, which was an affront to his dignity, to the picture of himself that ran and smudged.

Two bass notes are plucked, ascending minor to major, and the song circles back around the same words, but the early wistful mantra has become an absolute fucking banger with a hailstorm of John Reynolds's drums. This woman unleashes her fury and joy from the back of her throat, grounding this anthem in the very guts of her own survival. Eighteen years after I first heard the song, it would be on repeat on CD and I would be driving north from Georgia to New York City and positively flailing in my seat. Free. Free, yes, but with thirteen more years where visitation and exchanges were made where I wasn't present, where the man I dated and married and his parents stepped in to hand off my son while I hid nearby, where we bore the weight of scorn and the threat of something going awry.

The banger is that I got *out*. The banger is that I did it. The banger is that, as Sinéad hoots, her voice gets low and intimate and gravelly and you can hear she's herself. The banger is that I made myself into the person that continued to support his relationship with his child, that I never bad-mouthed him to our child, that I did everything I could to support my child's well-being. That I keep that binder and found EMDR and all the other treatments for C-PTSD that I will need for the rest of my life. The binder and the pound of flesh he took have made me into the person who will publish this essay, who will say it to the world. I am both deeply startled and flinching and fearless because I had to make myself into the person who could dance to the end of this song with a joy of knowing exactly who I am because of what I ran away from.

When Sinéad passed away, I was shocked. How could an element, the air we breathe, have died? Had I taken her for granted? The thread of her songs and her life and her joy and suffering were snipped and flailing in the wind and I could not hold the end of my own thread, a tense plucked guitar string. Michael Stipe shared on social media a version of the song he'd played in concert in 1996, the meaning now tripled as a mourning song, the last day of our acquaintance on this earth.

A few days later in a stunned upswelling of loss that shattered so many, I put on Spotify and this song came on and as I drove down I-95 I listened to it again and again on repeat, being launched by the ending, dancing and head banging in my seat as I sped south, and it was as though every single repeat was a surprise, the explosion in the story of my life. As I drove in a concrete channel surrounded with glassed towers of offices with wires strung above them, I wanted this song, and I needed other writers to choose theirs, and then when I got to the airport to pick up my mom I would post a few sentences on Facebook about the idea and it turned out that hundreds of people, too, had the song, the one song of many songs, each the essence of a flame we were lucky to have been lit by that told us the truth that no one else would.

To Go Without

"I Do Not Want What I Haven't Got"

STACEY LYNN BROWN

I am old enough now to have cycled through many seasons, to have struck out for, settled, and left behind many geographies, both mental and physical, and to have returned to what had once been familiar and find it almost unrecognizably changed. To find myself the same kind of stranger.

Landscapes change day to day, year to year, in both natural and unnatural ways, and a place, once left, is never the same upon return. Once left, a place ceases to exist and enters the domain of imagination, (re)constructed, as it is, through the lenses of distance, nostalgia, regret. And the person who did the leaving? They, too, become a construct, an afterimage of who they were before, tempered by what they have, and have yet to, become.

But a text of any sort—a photograph, a painting, a song—is frozen in time. Stilled. Taken out of the entirety of its context and put into a forever kind of parentheses where it is bracketed and preserved. It does not change from listen to listen or from view to view. But oh, how we do.

Certain songs are the mile markers of my life, capable of meaning wholly new and different things as I return to them, changing and changed by the time that has elapsed. A shuffling feed of versions of me contained in whatever my casing looks like at the time: larger or thinner, baby-faced or graying. They show me the distance of travel, both the glimpse from the rearview mirror as well as the spanning expanse that lies ahead. The totality of the horizon surrounds.

"I Do Not Want What I Haven't Got" is one of these songs, appearing, as it did, just as my relationship with my mother, and with mothering, was about to be irreversibly changed. It would be years before I learned the story behind the song—that it was written after she visited a psychic medium, eighteen months after her abusive mother had been killed in a car crash. Her daughters had refused her plea for forgiveness just before she died. The night of the visit to the medium, her mother appeared in a dream to Sinéad, speaking those words as if to make peace with the peace she was denied.

It would be years before I forgave my mother. First, I had to find out what she had done.

1990: I am nineteen, working in a music store, when Sinéad's second record drops. Unpacking the publicity materials, I slide the rolled-up poster from the cardboard tubing and unscroll the spotlit beauty of her face, the title handwritten beneath it like a captioned photograph in a family album. Such a far cry from the fisted armor and fearsome scream captured on her first cover. But I know looks can be deceiving. I have already had violence visited upon me in many guises, both soft and terrible. My mother is alive and lives across town. I see her when I need to do my laundry or want a homecooked meal. Every inch the ungrateful college kid.

I listen to this CD on repeat, just as I did The Lion and the Cobra. *Things are different for Sinéad now. You can feel it. She is stepping into her own light, emerging from the shadows of systemic and personified abuse. Bolder. More empowered. Her version of a Prince song will quickly become one of the best-selling songs of the year, far better than his own. But the track I listen to again and again is the title song, positioned, as it is, as both the end note of the album as well as the center of its gravity, holding the heavy weight of its story, a dramatic ending to the mapped journey of anger, regret, and grief.*

2000: The world does not end at midnight on New Year's Eve after all, and we all seem a little confused about what to do now. I have been helping a lover die, unmindful of much else. Soon, my niece will be born, convincing me I do, in fact, want kids. My hesitance will not have been about population control, as I told myself, but about my relationship with my own mother, first complicated by that which I had not known and then by the knowing itself, the truth always clawing its way out of whatever box or coffin it was buried in. And when ours is exhumed, when the story that cleaved her is finally brought into the light, the mother I knew disintegrates before my eyes, leaving behind bones and fragments I am left to rearrange into a shape that is somehow recognizable. The veil finally lifted from my eyes, I dress her in a shroud of her own making, presentable at last.

Without any other instruments to buoy the song or distract the listener, a cappella songs rely wholly on the nuances accomplished by the human voice, weaving in and out of silence, alternately occupying and vacating, interrupting and lingering, notes hovering in space like laundry pinned to the line. The voice alone creates the melody, creates, then often violates, expectations. The more you listen, the more you hear the nuances and subtext, both narratively as well as emotionally. This is anger, we know. This, grief. Wistfulness. And here is where power lies to be (re)claimed, as there is nothing this world finds more terrifying than a woman with a microphone.

2010: I have a five-year-old daughter whose abusive father drank. I will divorce too late to shield her from the damage I knew he was capable of, too soon for her to not internalize it as being about her lovability, her worthiness. My father has had a massive stroke and has lost both his language as well as his mobility, and my relationship with my mother, which had been strengthened by our therapy sessions, is being pulled taut again, fraying at the edges as she strains against the confines of her new reality in unwilling service: grounded, trapped, and grim.

When recording an a cappella song, the artist and producer have many aesthetic choices to make, including what to do about the breath. In the midst of otherwise silence, without the instruments that usually conceal, the breaths between notes become visible, a stitched garment turned over to reveal the underside's ragged seams. Whisking away the tablecloth, the art is left bare, stripped of its artifice unless edited out. In this song, Sinéad's breath is audible, the gasping, deep inhalations signaling both the ending of the previous phrase and the beginning of what is to come. A singer has to think a few measures ahead, to draw breath even when their lungs are still half-filled so as to be able to last, to give what must be given. To sustain and be sustained.

2020: My father will die just before Christmas, my mother ten months later. Neither a surprise. But no matter how aware you are of the inevitability and imminence, you can never really be prepared, as losing a parent is unlike anything else: how do you wake up on a planet that no longer contains them. How do you move, walk, think, talk in such an alien landscape day after day after day. The spoken, the unspoken, and the unheard are the only things made permanent in this lesson of impermanence, so many possibilities forever foreclosed. By the time they actually die, I have already lost them both, my father silently, stubbornly dragging the petrified wood of his body for a dozen years, and my mother's memory and understanding of the world incrementally stolen from her in small sips. Critical illness strips you down to your essence, distills you to who you fundamentally are. A journey of dissolution, this circular return to innocence and helplessness.

The song lyrics have a dreamlike quality and logic to them, skipping landscapes and perspectives, a parable that represents both itself as well as deeper truths. The singer has been prepared for the journey ahead by her mother. Because she is prepared, and has what is required, she is not frightened. Early in the journey, she sees a bluebird that advises her to take risks, to not try to be too pure, to fly closer to the sea. Later, she comes to understand that the bluebird was her, speaking wisdom across time and space to an earlier version of herself. And she is sated. Filled. Grateful for what she has and not in need of anything she does not. This, the happiness. This, the key.

2024: My dead mother comes to me in a dream. In that blue-gray gauze between sleep and full consciousness, when I know I am awake but have not yet opened my eyes, I can see her standing by my bed, wearing the housecoat of my elementary school years, the years she mothered me most. Years when her stilted attempts to give care, limited to thermometers and glasses of ginger ale, were gobbled up gratefully. She watches over me, a concerned and fretful look on her face. I watch her there for a moment, almost comforted, before reaching for her, but the moment my mind mouths *Mom*, she is sucked backward and away from me in a violent diminishing, extending her arms toward me even as the rest of her disappears, reaching out to me through space and time as if to finally hold me. As if we both might finally be held.

Ultimately, an a cappella song is an act of faith, both in exhalation as story and in the listener's willingness to follow breath wherever it may lead. Every journey ends in the same place, and we wait our turn to follow, no matter how much we miss the traveler who walks ahead. That which was exhumed returns with my mother to the earth. The song remains unchanged. I ache and wail and learn how to go without. And though I may no longer need, I will always, always want.

You Are Something

"Don't Cry for Me Argentina"

MIEKE EERKENS

I.

When I was a teenager, I saw Sinéad O'Connor driving in my hometown of Los Angeles. She was behind the wheel of a white BMW, her windows open to let the warm afternoon in.

I loved Sinéad at that time. I had spent high school pacing the deck at swim meets with her impassioned songs coming through my headphones as I psyched myself up for my races. I drove up the Pacific Coast Highway with my best friend, windows down, Sinéad howling "oh-ho-ho" into the briny wind at the climax of a song that had begun as barely a whisper. This was her appeal, the delicious dramatic juxtaposition of frail and fierce, soft and hard, docile and ferocious.

I loved her because I was an idealist who wanted to fix the broken world, too. I believed in her dedication to the poor, the abused, the marginalized. Sinéad spoke of her rejection of material success and had stated that she did not measure her career by the money her music earned, but by how well she stayed true to her beliefs and connected with her fans in live performance. And I was a passionate young person with uncompromising ideals that I would only learn later in life were difficult to meet. Her brazen rejection of the systems of power that other artists feared to challenge thrilled me.

So seeing the renegade Sinéad O'Connor tooling around Beverly Hills in a shiny white BMW—a car I associated with the excess and materialism of the upper class—was a moment of profound cognitive dissonance. As an adult, of course I understand that the BMW was most likely a rental car arranged by an assistant at the record label and not something she chose. Or even if it was something she chose, driving a fancy car did not cancel out her ideals. But as a teen I did not know anything about anything, and I was upset. I said to my friend at a not insignificant volume, "Wow. Look at that. Sinéad O'Connor drives a white BMW. Don't you think that kind of makes her a fucking hypocrite? What a sellout." And Sinéad, who was stopped at the light right next to us, turned and looked at me through the open window with such a genuine look of confusion and hurt that I immediately regretted it. She had heard me. And to be honest, I think I had wanted her to hear me. No, that's a lie; I know I had wanted her to hear me.

II.

On the day I learned Sinéad O'Connor was dead, I watched video after video of her performing her most famous songs, but the video that brought me into an ugly cry was a live performance of "Don't Cry for Me Argentina," a cover of the song from the musical *Evita* that appeared on her 1992 album *Am I Not Your Girl?* The album itself distanced Sinéad from the wild success of the edgy *I Do Not Want What I Haven't Got*, as she turned away from the superstardom and controversy of that album to return to the comfort of the songs she grew up listening to and singing in pubs. The album was a record scratch on the momentum of her career, but for her, it was a repatriation. "Don't Cry for Me Argentina" was a musical homecoming.

I had never seen her perform the song. To me it perfectly captured the warring forces inside Sinéad. Written by Andrew Lloyd Webber and Tim Rice, the song appears in *Evita* twice, initially from the perspective of the ghost of Eva Perón, the former first lady of Argentina and protagonist of the musical, and later in full as a powerful living woman addressing her country. I had not known, but learned in the process of researching the song, that Lloyd Webber intended the word "cry" to be interpreted as "weeping" from the perspective of the ghost, but in the context of the speech as first lady, the word could also be interpreted as "shouting" or "calling out." This fact strikes me as fitting. Weeping and shouting are the duality that lived inside Sinéad. Often seen as a defiant, powerful woman like Eva Perón, Sinéad embodied the other side of that defiance in her rendition of the song, which reflects a quiet and sorrowful yearning. In the video of her performance, her voice is soft and childlike, a plea. She makes the song her own, the lyrics no longer Evita's but hers.

Every time I see this performance, I see it through a different interpretive lens.

III.

In her memoir and in interviews, Sinéad references singing "Don't Cry for Me Argentina" as a child for her mother. In an interview before a performance of the song on a Dutch talk show, Sinéad smiles sheepishly when the interviewer says, "It's a song that has got a very special meaning for you, I think?" "Oh, because I used to sing it to my mummie," she answers, infused with love. Her face transforms into that of the child Sinéad on the word *mummie*, and she glances downward in memory before looking back at the interviewer with a sheepish expression, almost as if she's confessing an embarrassing secret. "I used to sing [it] in talent competitions and in hotels, and win the fiver." She is lost in the memory for a moment, proud. Her mother taught her to steal from the collection plate at church, after all.

It might be perplexing from the outside to see this kind of daughterly devotion when Sinéad often described her mother as a cruel sadist, a woman who beat her daily and made her strip naked as she stomped on her abdomen, trying to destroy her reproductive organs. She told Sinéad she was worthless and made her repeat, "I am nothing, I am nothing, I am nothing." She made Sinéad sleep in the garden shed or locked her in a dark room for a whole weekend. She subjected Sinéad to constant physical, sexual, and emotional abuse, as Sinéad tells it. Sinéad described her as "evil" and "possessed."

And yet. The opposing force of love in Sinéad meant she remained devoted to and obsessed with her mother her entire life. "I hate not being able to love her . . . I would have taken care of her even though she was an absolute monster. . . . My life has been terrible, terrible, terrible, but I miss her so bad. I can't wait to see her again," she said in an interview in 2017. When Sinéad was eighteen, her mother died in a car accident. Her yearning for the maternal love that she never got, as well as the yearning to make her mother whole, would remain permanently unresolved. Now she'd never be able to convince her mother she wasn't nothing. Per Sinéad, "Nothing could ever be fixed again or will ever be fixed again."

I am profoundly moved by her ability to hold these dichotomous feelings simultaneously. Here is where I think the heart of the artist Sinéad lay, and how this song speaks to her complicated relationship with the world. I know this relationship. A mother wound permeates every subsequent relationship; it is a void that will not be filled, a despairing desire for love, an indefatigable wish to heal the damaged world as one wishes she could heal the mother. By the artist's own admission, this mother wound imbues every Sinéad O'Connor song and performance. It's what draws me to this song, a song that is for me inextricably linked with the mother wound, because "I am something, I am something, I am something" all comes down to "love me, love me, love me." And Sinéad's version of "Don't Cry for Me Argentina" is as much about this vulnerable plea to the public as it is about the rebellion and strength that also lived in Sinéad O'Connor. And in me. Love me in spite of my anger, my depression, my faults. The wounded mother relationship is projected onto our relationship with the world. I see it there at the beginning of the song:

It won't be easy, you'll think it strange
When I try to explain how I feel
That I still need your love after all that I've done

I also can't help but contemplate whether the persona of Sinéad's mother's ghost inhabits those words, too, a wish projected onto the song's narrator by Sinéad. She spoke of how much she wanted to be able to love her mother, to forgive her and view her cruelty as a product of her own wounds. Needing Sinéad's love after all her mother had done to her would have been a salve to Sinéad's soul. In the mind of the child of the wounded mother, being needed equates to being loved. Sinéad could recognize her damaged mother's need for love and forgiveness because of her own deep need for love and forgiveness. That's the legacy of trauma.

IV.

I watch the video of the performance again. Like turning a gemstone, the light catches and reflects a new color each time. The lyrics become something new.

During the period that she promoted the album on which her rendition of "Don't Cry for Me Argentina" appeared, many in the public and music industry turned their backs on her after Sinéad defiantly ripped up a photo of the pope that had belonged to her mother on live television in protest of child abuse by the Catholic Church. I see this version of her in the lines:

I had to let it happen, I had to change
Couldn't stay all my life down at heel

The performance of "Don't Cry for Me Argentina" that I watched happened post-scandal, and her rendition takes on new meaning with the knowledge of how terribly she had been treated for speaking the truth. It doesn't matter that she was right and would be vindicated a decade later. She was cast out, and her career never fully recovered. Sinéad indicated in many interviews that she didn't mind the loss of fame. But I think the loss of the public's love was different. I imagine the public's rejection of her principled stand clawed open old wounds. It is this part of her history that I project onto this viewing of her performance of "Don't Cry for Me Argentina."

The truth is, I never left you
All through my wild days, my mad existence
I kept my promise
Don't keep your distance

I see the Sinéad who sings these lines as someone carrying the pain of being profoundly misunderstood by the masses and asking the public to come back to her. But for many years they didn't come back.

V.

The lens changes again on another viewing as I think of the middle-aged Sinéad, the depressed Sinéad in the years before her death.

In the decades that she faded from the public eye and was replaced by new musical talents, her depression brought her to the ground repeatedly. She spoke of suicide. She converted to Islam, and posted long rants and grievances about never wanting to spend time with white people again or finding anyone who wasn't Muslim disgusting, before recanting and apologizing. She created, then deleted, then re-created social media accounts under various names: Magda Davitt. Shuhada Sadaqat. Then back to Sinéad O'Connor. She accused her family of kidnapping her son, made paranoid proclamations.

At a low point in 2017, she posted a video on her social media account in which she cried alone in a motel in New Jersey, speaking of suicidal ideation and loneliness. The video was heartrending. I have struggled with depression and deep loneliness for most of my life, and her desperation for relief was familiar. She acknowledged that she was difficult, that she could be a burden, but that she wanted to show the kind of struggle that millions of people with mental illness experience. She lamented that so often they are left to suffer alone, having worn out the patience of their loved ones with repeated incidents.

And it's easy to see why her family and close friends may have distanced themselves from her at that point, if what she said was true. Sinéad had been diagnosed with borderline personality disorder and bipolar disorder by at least one doctor. She struggled with addiction. She posted angry rants online about her family. Continuing a relationship with a volatile, highly emotional person whom you love can be absolute hell. None of that changes the fact that Sinéad O'Connor was in pain and was worthy of love and support.

So I was thrilled to see that she was making a comeback and performing again after getting professional help. In 2019, I posted a clip to my social media of Sinéad in her comeback performance on Ireland's *Late Late Show*, singing "Nothing Compares 2 U" in a headscarf, with her eyes shut the entire time, opening them only at the end to turn to the band and flash a brilliant, triumphant smile.

The next time I watch the performance of "Don't Cry for Me Argentina" the gemstone catches new light and it is this Sinéad whose voice I hear inside the lyrics, though this version of Sinéad came into being long after the performance was recorded. For me it's a retroactive interpretation, the young Sinéad singing as a future version of herself.

I still need your love after all that I've done

The next day, the headlines were decisive. "Sinéad O'Connor Melts Hearts on Late Late Show." "Sinéad O'Connor Makes Stunning TV Comeback." "Sinéad O'Connor Delivers Epic Comeback Performance."

VI.

The day she died I watched that video over and over, projected all of these versions of Sinéad O'Connor onto this achingly vulnerable performance and cried. But each of these versions of her that informed my interpretation as an adult in 2023—the Sinéad with the mother wound, the rejected Sinéad, the misunderstood Sinéad, the tentative comeback Sinéad—was framed by the memory of that moment on a Los Angeles street that still makes me flush with shame.

And as for fortune, and as for fame
I never invited them in
Though it seemed to the world they were all I desired

When I saw Sinéad earnestly singing these lines with that same wounded look on her face as I had seen decades earlier as she sat in that BMW, it was as though she was singing those lyrics to me.

Even in the moment I immediately had wished I could unsay the thing: "What a sellout." The light turned green. Sinéad turned her face back to the traffic and drove away. And while she probably forgot about it ten seconds later, I have always remembered that, for a moment, I was just another person who misunderstood and rejected her. It wasn't that I felt I had any importance to Sinéad O'Connor. I was one of a million strangers. This is about me and my perception of myself. It was a moment between us in which I failed to be better than the masses who hurt her. I had cast my stone to fall upon a mountain of stones around her. And even now in the shame of this teenage memory I wish I could spool back time like a movie reel, to remove this tiny cut from the film of a person who felt misunderstood her whole life.

I love you, and hope you love me, Sinéad sings, and I hear the lyrics as Sinéad's appeal to an asshole kid with her own mother wound.

> *Have I said too much?*
> *There's nothing more I can think of to say to you*
> *But all you have to do is look at me to know*
> *That every word is true*

On the day Sinéad O'Connor died, I saw a spectrum of her manifestations in this world contained in the words of a song she sang to me from the past. But every single version of her seemed to want the same thing. It was only in her death that I saw it so clearly. How I wish on that 1990s streetcorner I could have instead told the young version of her what I felt welling in me when I watched her perform this song on repeat the day she died. "Sinéad, you are something, you are something, you are something, you are something."

I Say War

"War"

STEPHANIE ELIZONDO GRIEST

The clinking began in the back of the ballroom. Forks struck glasses, repeatedly. From whom, I could not see. The stage lights illumined only my closest audience members. They craned their necks, looking for the source of the sound, seemingly as puzzled as me. Not yet grasping the connection between this sound and my text, I kept reading. The forks, meanwhile, kept clinking.

This wasn't just the fanciest dinner at which I had (or would ever) read; it was also the fanciest dinner I had (or would ever) attend. Tickets started at $350. Among the guests I'd met were oilmen, bankers, publishers, and politicians. The men wore Lucchese s, the thousand-dollar version of the boots my *tios* donned for ranch work. Their wives wore diamonds or pearls. Hailing from the part of Texas where "black tie" meant quinceañera attire, I had opted for a dress that a fairy might don to dance flamenco. It was red to symbolize the subjects of my book: Russia, China, and Cuba. As the clinking grew louder, my face turned the same color.

"Should I stop?" I asked.

From the front row, a bald man in a tuxedo mouthed "NO." He

waved me on encouragingly. I picked up where I had left off, but the clinking had grown so insistent, I could barely hear myself. And then came the rumble, a throaty torrent that seemed to ricochet off the walls of the ballroom. My thoughts first darted to my parents, seated somewhere in the darkness. They were so proud that I had finally published the book I'd moved back in with them to write. I couldn't let them watch their daughter get booed by three hundred people. The other authors in attendance also came to mind, one of whom was my literary idol. She shouldn't be witnessing this, either.

So, I skipped from the middle of the passage to the very end, read it fast, and stepped down from the stage. The few people I could make out were standing, as if in ovation, but the booing had reached a fever pitch. A man wearing a Stetson threw his arms around me. "Don't you listen to what anybody says, you were great," he drawled through whiskey breath.

Breaking free, I ducked into the nearest bathroom and locked myself inside a stall. Where did I go wrong? The two authors who preceded me on stage, decades-older white men, had read about the glories of Texas. I read about the rumba queens of Havana. Was that it? No. The audience's energy had shifted before I even started reading. I distinctly heard guffaws during my introduction of my work, when I derided the U.S. trade embargo against Cuba and President George W. Bush's ongoing policies there. That must have been it. This was, after all, 2004: his reelection year. This was, after all, Texas.

Anxiety gripped my chest. Would Random House drop me from their list? Had I—at age thirty—just ruined my career?

I emerged from the stall to find two wives in pearls refreshing their lipstick. They looked askance at me before leaving. As I washed my still-shaking hands, two younger women walked in. They promptly started comforting me.

"You were like . . . like . . . like *that bald chick*!" one said.

"Bald?" I asked.

"Yeah. That one who tore up the pope!"

With that invocation, my whole heart soared.

I was lucky to grow up with an older sister with discerning taste. She brought home U2's *Under a Blood Red Sky* when I was eight and played it repeatedly. I didn't catch any of Bono's references but enjoyed quoting "Sunday Bloody Sunday" on the playground. "Broken bottles under children's feet!" I screamed from the swings. "Bodies strewn across a dead-end street!" When a teacher finally explained The Troubles of Northern Ireland to me, an inner light bulb flicked on. My reading material had yet to evolve beyond Beverly Cleary, so music became my entrée to the global world. Midnight Oil's "Beds Are Burning" taught me about Aboriginal land rights; Steven Van Zandt's "Sun City" is how I learned about apartheid. Bob Marley opened my eyes to colonial transgressions. When the liner notes of U2's latest album said to join Amnesty International, I did. The inherent hope of writing letters to free political prisoners as a teenager is no doubt what led me to pursue social justice as a journalist in adulthood.

Sinéad O'Connor burst onto the scene when I was in high school. With her shaved head and howling lyrics, she epitomized the righteous indignation I felt on behalf of the planet. I blasted *I Do Not Want What I Haven't Got* as I drove to the mall to fold Gap jeans for $4.15 an hour, berating Margaret Thatcher all the while. Unlike the other musicians I worshipped, Sinéad was a woman, which made her work not just inspirational but aspirational. She shaped my whole understanding of art, not just what it *could* do, but what it *should* do.

So, I was among the many fans who cheered that night in 1992 when she stepped onto the *Saturday Night Live* stage wearing a dress of white lace. My elation escalated when she gripped the microphone wrapped in Rasta cloth and launched into an a cappella rendition of my favorite Bob Marley song—the one composed out of a speech Ethiopian emperor Haile Selassie once delivered to the United Nations. Midway through, however, Sinéad changed a key lyric of "War" so that "Africans" became "children." Then, she brandished a photograph. I leaned into the television screen. *El papa?* Suddenly, Sinéad was shredding him to pieces. "Fight the real enemy," she declared before blowing out a tray of candles.

Like most Chicanas, I was raised Catholic, and like most Tejanas, I adored Pope John Paul II. Not only was he the first pope in history to visit Mexico (five times!), but he came to see us in South Texas, too. More than 300,000 devotees crammed onto a San Antonio field to greet him, my rosary-reciting *tias* among them. They had wept when he addressed the crowd in Spanish; when he implored Texans to "show mercy" to Mexican immigrants; when he lauded Mexican loyalty to family.

Desecrating the single most powerful man to ever speak up on behalf of my beleaguered community, then, was a little too radical for my eighteen-year-old sensibilities. I hadn't studied the conquest of Mexico yet. I didn't know what Catholic doctrine meant for gay people yet, or for anyone needing reproductive care. The *Boston Globe* was still a decade away from publishing its Pulitzer Prize–winning investigation of priests who'd sexually preyed upon children. The Polish press was still three decades away from scrutinizing Pope John Paul II's role in the cover-up.

Which is to say: I was among the many fans who abandoned Sinéad that night.

Two days after getting booed on a ballroom stage, I flew home to Brooklyn, tossed aside my suitcases, and crumpled onto my bedroom floor. My career was over. I was sure of it. At some point in the pity party that ensued, I reached for my box of old cassette tapes. Music is what ignited my political consciousness in the first place. Perhaps it could offer direction now that I'd experienced its consequences—or at least some solace?

Popping vintage U2 into the tape deck sat me upright. Bob Marley got me grooving. When his opening chords to "War" jangled through the speakers, I remembered those ladies in the bathroom. Dipping back into the box, I found *I Do Not Want What I Haven't Got* and cranked up the volume. The sound of Sinéad whispering the Serenity Prayer got me crying, but by "I Am Stretched on Your Grave," I was dancing. Does anything slay demons like her angel-scream? I flipped that tape again and again as I exorcised that terrible night out of my system.

The next morning, I scoured the internet. Because I'm a masochist, my first search was to see if anyone had written about my public humiliation. Social media hadn't taken off yet, so the coverage was mercifully minimal. One blogger said the attendees booed because I was overly emphatic. *About a trade embargo that deprives 11 million people of food and medicine?* Another said I talked too much. *About a trade embargo that deprives 11 million people of food and medicine?*

My second search was for stories about the night Sinéad got booed. I remembered reading about it in *Rolling Stone* after it happened, but I was awed nonetheless by my findings.

Two weeks after the 1992 *SNL* fiasco, Sinéad arrived at Madison Square Garden to pay tribute to her childhood idol, Bob Dylan, alongside the biggest names in the business. Johnny Cash. Lou Reed. Stevie Wonder. Willie Nelson. George Harrison. Neil Young. Tom Petty. Tracy Chapman. Some 18,000 fans packed the arena to hear their renditions of Dylan's most iconic songs, which cameras live-casted around the globe.

Sinéad chose a turquoise overcoat with Napoleonic buttons for the occasion. All smiles when she stepped on the stage, she was visibly stunned when her applause got overwhelmed by a sound she later described as a "thunderclap that never ends." For an extended moment, she just stood and blinked as the jeers filled the arena. But when the pianist played the opening bars to Dylan's "I Believe in You," Sinéad threw her arms out perpendicular to her body, as if to physically block the music. Kris Kristofferson—her Stetson man—raced over. "Don't let the bastards get you down."

"I'm not down," she purportedly said.

From there, Sinéad paced the stage, her hands behind her back. No doubt, she was thinking about her father, sitting in the dark of the arena. She probably thought about Dylan, her hero, too. The pianist, meanwhile, resumed playing. The booing was bloodthirsty by this point. Sinéad allowed another thirty seconds to pass before she turned to the pianist and drew her index finger across her neck. Grabbing the mic, she yelled: "Okay, turn this up."

Facing a sonic riot with nothing but righteousness for protection, Sinéad ripped the monitors out of her ears before shout-growling another a cappella version of "War."

Until the philosophy . . .

She slung each word like a hatchet. Every time you thought she'd quit, she soldiered through another verse. People remember Sinéad getting "booed off the stage," but no. She made it through two-thirds of the song before throwing down her gauntlet.

Everywhere is war!

For the next five seconds, she stared daggers at 18,000 screaming people. Only then did she retreat. People have written about her running off crying to Kristofferson, but the footage clearly shows him reaching for her first. "It just seemed to me wrong, booing that little girl out there," he later said on Irish TV.

Sinéad was twenty-six at the time. She was the mother of a four-year-old. She was a multiplatinum, Grammy and MTV Music Video Award–winning composer, musician, and performer. She was neither "a bald chick" nor a "little girl." She was a woman with conviction.

It has been twenty years since I got booed on a ballroom stage. Contrary to my fears, my ego has been the only casualty. (A writer I once admired still pointedly asks about that night every time he sees me.) Random House did drop me from their list, but book sales were probably the culprit.

Crowds booing artists have only grown more pervasive in our culture, not to mention more dangerous. An audience member threw a bottle of urine at Cher Lloyd during her performance at V Festival in 2012. Seven years later, Ariana Grande got pelted by a lemon. Four years after that, Bebe Rexha got stitches after being struck in the eye by a flying cell phone. Ten days after that, Kelsea Ballerini got hit in the face by a projectile bracelet.

Sinéad maintained that her booing did not derail her career but rather re-railed it. In her 2021 memoir *Rememberings*, she wrote: "Some things are worth losing your career for."

As vehemently as I disagreed with the U.S. trade embargo against Cuba, I was truthfully not, at age thirty, ready to lose my career over it. My time, yes. My ego: sure. But writing was my whole purpose for being. I found deeper convictions when I moved to Mexico to research my next book, and even more when I relocated back to South Texas for the book after that. Today when I give readings about the humanitarian crisis at the U.S.–Mexico border, I am unafraid to sling hatchets of my own, regardless of the consequences.

This, to me, is the legacy of Sinéad O'Connor. For what will you be booed—and keep on singing? For what will you keep on writing and speaking? For what will you say *war*?

patron saint

"Thank You for Hearing Me"

LEAH LAKSHMI PIEPZNA-SAMARASINHA

picture this: it's 2002 or 2003. you are a feral skinny young light brown nerd femme thing, scrawny with the sticking out light brown chicken collarbones under your hoodie and all your waffle knits and littletiny strappy tank tops from the sale rack of the urban outfitters. you are layered TF up because you live in Toronto and for the purposes of this story it is February and it has been minus 18 for a really long time. your construction boots from the store that sells to people who do manual labor in kensington, like you do. the clothes you scavenge. you are a scavenger. you are a scavenged thing.

you're in your basement bachelor (that's what canadians call a studio, like everyone who's broke is a tv lady's man) apartment at davenport and shaw. the apartment has a lot to not recommend it: you stare up at exposed pipes every morning and night, there's only three small half windows in the whole thing and they all look out at ground zero of the side of the house next door. so not only might you die if there's a fire and not only could someone (say, your ex, your parents) break in with ease, it's dark as hell and toronto has a seven-month cold season. you have four or five lamps with bulbs from the No Frills going at all times but the No Frills bulbs aren't the best so they keep burning out.

also: a futon not from the trash that was your big investment, an altar on a fruit crate with the image of Durga someone left in the garbage at your old apartment building, a shitty built-in particle board bookshelf where your books are so buxom the shelves bell way far south in the middle. no tub and that's the worst part—you would die for a bath when you hurt, and you are in early crip so you hurt all the fucking time, but there's just a crappy plastic shower insert whose sides also bow out.

but it is four hundred and seventy-five dollars a month inclusive. that's it, the whole thing. and it's all yours and the door locks. no matter how sick or crazy you are that month you can usually scrape up four hundred and seventy-five dollars. also your landlady is the daughter of a guy who runs a corner store in Parkdale, she's in engineering school on the Canadian immigrant dream and took her OSAP and used it to put a down payment on this house. she's only two years younger than you which makes you feel like shit, but it also means she is realll understanding when you "forget" to pay for ten days.

you sit in your basement in between working housecleaning gigs (at the terrible "eco cleaner" run by a white lez from South Africa who takes half your check, but you look too crazy to get your own gigs scrubbing the clawfoots of the rich and reno'd), in between landscaping and later working the rape crisis line and then the psychic hot line when the rape crisis lays you off, and triking to the club because despite it all you are still trying to be some kind of queer in your twenties.

you are some kind of queer in your twenties but you are also not like the others of them because you need a lot of rest, like 18 hours a day of chronically ill rest. you fill journals with every single broken glass thing. you have a safety plan from not just your ex but also from your parents. you are an incest survivor which is sort of comprehensible but when you say it's your mom the pin just drops.

you are underground. this is where poor people are consigned to live in toronto, in canada, in basements. sometimes, often, you dream of even a ground floor apartment, sunlight, a bathtub, heat you control.

but sometimes you like living underground, unseen. sometimes you lose your shit because you may have looked twenty-five when you were fourteen but you're still fucking young and trauma cooks in you and bursts like a chestburster, like infection that hasn't been cleaned all the way out yet and dressed with a proper dressing, needs to get out.

that's why this place with its pipes and its cheap rent you can manage to pay even if you're really sick or crazy this month, it's your palace. here you can be alone and crazy and unperceived. chest burst your bad shit when it swells out. making your bones in the dark. a survivor. surviving.

This is the after. You're living in the after.

there's a small brown brick chipped blue-paint ramp library branch on the corner, it kind of matches the small Portuguese grocery store around the corner from that, a little bigger than a bodega, that has oil and pasta and milk and bread and some crates of onions and lemons and potatoes. they're both a block away, so you can get there when you don't have money for the bus, when it's too cold to trike, when your legs are too fucking wobbly and your ass hurts too much, when you can't brain manage the people going to the No Frills in the dufferin mall or the IGA down on dupont.

the library is small and not the best but has a ramp and its smallness makes it manageable when you are having a day where you can't deal with big. they have some old favorites, spines fingered and cracked soft under their plastic covers. they can receive the hold requests you put in. they have cds on spinner racks. sometimes you check shit out impulsively. one day, you grab sinéad's double live cd, *she who dwells*. you feel embarrassed even though nobody at the shaw and davenport tiny branch is going to judge you. you feel embarrassed like you did when you bought hole's *pretty on the inside* tape from Tower when you were nineteen because it wasn't a 7-inch vinyl hardcore band bought off a blanket at the ABC No Rio show. but also because it was some kind of slutty freak girl screaming or singing beautifully or both, about shit that happened to her. I listened to it in that basement.

thank you for hearing me
thank you for loving me

What is that if not the simplest survivor prayer?

thank you for seeing me
and for not leaving me

Thanks for hearing what I said. Not leaving me once you heard it—no abandonment.

Thank you for staying with me
Thanks for not hurting me

Thanks for not hurting me—maybe you were the first one. Loving me, which is all of those things.

all the stuff that should be like, *of course*. But isn't.

A survivor in the basement, hearing the repetition of that prayer: *thank you for hearing me, loving me, seeing me, not leaving me.*

The simplest purest thanks in my heart for the people who were doing that, for the first time since I got free.

And the childlike wonder at, *this is possible*?

Underneath, the infinity ten thousand mirror grief understory of, *this was always possible*.

When Sinéad died, you cried and pawed through all her songs on youtube. Texted a lover that you wanted to get the whole of the emperor's new clothes tattooed on your thigh and they were like, *maybe just one line*. you settled for *you asked for the truth and I told you* on your right thigh. simple.

you want that tat to hold you up, your thick right thigh with its curly sri lankan trail of curls on the inside, and then your whole body. the naked stark of those words. In the middle of a protracted legal battle with the executor of your mother's estate. your mother who inexplicably left you the house money that was her working class femme life's inheritance. she couldn't say your name in the will but she still left you her palace, the house every penny she sweated out had gone into. the safe place she could be crazy in, the dangerous place because the wound not healed exploded pus. the executor is enraged at you because you are a bad survivor girl who inexplicably grew up and wrote shit about your life that people inexplicably liked, and he goes so far as to xerox pages from your memoir and submit it in probate as some kind of delulu but so regular old white man ranting about how you are some kind of bad lying freak crazy slut saying things that didn't happen and you don't deserve what your mother left you.

oh Sinéad, you knew that survivor femme queer slut shut the fuck up crazy bitch shame, except you got it from the whole ass entire world, you got it from a million people in concert halls. you were that inexplicable thing, the voice of an archangel demon godx coming out of that throat that just wants to sing. who then doesn't shut up after she's just sung a pretty heartbreak song on command and for profit.

you did a wholeass spell, Sinéad, a curse breaking, when you tore up that rapist pederast's photo on *Saturday Night Live*. mom cursed you out, it was so rude of her, hmmmph. mama who whispered to me about what the catholic church of webster MA had done to her, the men of it. what her father did when he broke a yardstick on her. what happened in the basement. my grandfather, the son of a man who was expelled from ireland when the local gentry's daughter had an affair with a commoner and as punishment all the men of marriageable age were rounded up and given a choice: immigrate to america or australia. my grandfather who drank a fifth of vodka a day until he was informed it was liver cancer and he'd have to stop, and he had a heart attack that night in the hospital because life without booze wasn't possible to live. all the tremors ricocheting down. your mama hissed at Sinéad on the screen the way survivors will when they see someone, another survivor, who dares to do what they can't.

When your mom dies, it's twenty-five years since you were in that basement Toronto runaway shithole palace. you're grown. you made it, you repeat, you made it. you made it strong enough that you decided to come back to MA for the first time since you got the fuck out when you were eighteen, to hold vigil for her as she crosses over to the other side. you are in western mass, not worcester mass, but it's the same dirty river shitty bus cheap ice cream pothole ice rut descendants of pilgrims runways and migrants refugees stop and shop dunkie's floodplain smell route 9 reality, just with an overlay of liberal arts college kids and coexist bumper stickers. the same wet creek working class Nipmuc territory as grew your ma and you. where the hurt happened. where she left and came back and spent the last fifty-two years of her life and died. where you left as soon as you could and stayed away and came back when you were strong enough, to sing her to the other side, talk to her spirit from your couch.

it's a whole nother covid winter. it's almost thirty years later than when you were that scrawny chickenbone kid. you're in another semi crap apartment, second floor of a triple decker that smells like mildew and old fake wood paneling and colonial themed wallpaper in the hallway, literal pioneers in covered wagons with a big crack through the plaster. the cold comes through the old window panes. you lie on your hot pink velvet splurge couch and cradle your macbook air 11 incher on your chest and watch *nothing compares*. the movie tells you what you knew but you know more now: sinéad was molested by her mother, abused by the nuns at the magdalene laundries. an inheritor of the lineage of the british colonization of ireland, the breaking staff of the christian cross against the goddess snakes.

mother daughter, woman to girl incest runs like a silent loud river through all of us colonization survivors. and there's something about the working class catholic church that cements it. it comes out in stories out the sides of our mouth. there's something about the mother-root. something about who bears you and breaks you. something about the river of pain we ride out and if we're lucky, break it before we break ourselves or break it on another.

sinéad, patron saint of working class catholic mother daughter survivor girls. phoenix. sacrifice. you lived and I hope you had joy. you did a spell to free us. your whole life and art about survivor without mostly ever saying that word. you said it out the side of your mouth, full throat.

sometimes survivors survive and sometimes we die young and sometimes that doesn't negate our whole life we made:

thank you for breaking my heart
thank you for tearing me apart

sometimes our lives are still a crazy freedom spell that frees infinity others

now i've got a strong strong heart
thank you for breaking my heart

thank you.

St. Sinéad

"Famine"

LAURETTA HANNON

Insurgent.

Prophet.

Problem.

Badass.

Mental case.

Grenade lobber.

Dissident saint.

Call her anything you want, but one thing is certain: her eyes were always on God. And for anyone seeking to express her own truth—Sinéad reigns as master teacher and spiritual guardian.

Savannah, Georgia, 1994

At the first listen of "Famine," I sensed it had something for me. I had a dim inkling that I might one day write my memoir. I knew that the lies and putrid secrets of my family needed outing, but how would I go about it? Would it be worth the personal pain and the risk of my mother disowning me?

My beautiful, duplicitous mama had adhered to an alternate storyline when it came to her history and ours. This book would bust it wide open on page one.

Likewise, "Famine" bolts out of the gate by exposing a fallacy: the notion that an Irish potato famine killed at least 1 million Irish in the nineteenth century. In fact, they starved to death because the English exported all other food from the country. We already knew this in my family. Some of our ancestors were forced to eat grass, dying with their mouths ringed in green stain.

After its explosive opening, the song describes the festering boils caused by the deception and then details the steps required for the healing process. In short, Sinéad gifted me with a succinct manual for writing my truth.

"Famine" spells out a four-part method: Remember, Grieve, Gain Knowledge and Understanding, and Forgive. Following this raw, profound process might have taken a decade, but it ultimately gave me the cojones needed for my memoir. And in the telling of my story, I found the medicine for much of the trauma I'd experienced. The curative, as it turns out, was inside the wound all along.

1. Remember

Sinéad raps about the devastation that results when a people loses its history and memories of the truth of what happened. She compares the Irish to an abused child who "has to drive itself out of its head because it's frightened," a child who suffers torment without end. Generation after generation.

When we don't stop to remember, self-destruction supervenes. This behavior could involve the usual suspects of alcohol or drug addiction, as well as other forms of escape that never end well. You cannot outrun your pain. It is The Great Teacher and must be looked dead in the eye. Remembering begins to accomplish that.

So I sat down to recall everything I could from childhood, good or bad. My parents' drunken knock-down drag-outs (and the sick laughter erupting from them); Mama's nervous breakdown and hospitalization; the threat of being removed from my family by the state; my older sisters and what they went through; and lastly: the love that somehow still lived under our rotting, leaking roof, too.

When I asked my sisters about any of this, I got the same response: they didn't remember. Although they were eight and ten years older than me, they feigned amnesia. In an attempt to avoid the agony, they tried to black out the memories and refused to open up.

What was the outcome of their decision? Well, look no further than "Famine" for the clue. Both sisters became heavy users of booze, bottles stashed surreptitiously throughout their homes. One sister used crystal meth daily, for years. That sister was plagued nightly by dreams she dared not articulate. She died at fifty-two still believing she was unworthy and less than. In the last voicemail from her, she began her message like she had every other time:

"Retta, it's just me."

I had nightmares as well. The plotline never varied: demonic creatures would be coming for my body and soul. The sound of my scream would jolt me awake, upright in the bed like in a bad '80s music video. These night terrors ended when I stopped to remember, and to write about it.

2. Grieve

Once I sat with the memories, the sadness and loss pressed like juggernauts on my chest. All I wanted to do was flee from my writing shed and possibly burn it to the ground, but Sinéad said I must grieve. By this point, I'd recognized her, and more specifically "Famine," as my spiritual guide. So I cried, took long solitary drives, and frequented Waffle Houses to write out the feelings.

It's safe to do just about anything within the walls of a Waffle House. I could weep over my plate of scattered and smothered hash browns, and it didn't raise an eyebrow. As tears smeared the pink ink on my journal pages, no one bothered me or paid me any mind. In the amniotic cocoon of the all-night diner, I could open the vein. The toxins came out in rivers of words.

But even there I wouldn't write about the cataclysmic rupture in my life: my father's death when I was seventeen. He had been my only stability, and I was present when the heart attack seized him. This was the place I least wanted to revisit.

Although I knew I had to go there, I trumped-up all manner of absurd diversions to postpone the anguish. A trip to the mall to look at lipsticks. A deep-cleaning of the ceiling fans in the house. A plan to start walking one of my cats—a project ditched after extensive googling and fret over the potential stress it could cause kitty. After months of playing this game, I surrendered.

As I mourned the smoking wreckage of my childhood, I could detect an interior change underway. Flashes of insight came about the grown-ups and why they did what they did to us. I felt lighter and more accepting of what happened. Looking back, I was being primed for the next phase.

3. Gain Knowledge and Understanding

Once I remembered and grieved my suffering, a door opened to wisdom and tenderness toward *most* everyone concerned. I didn't get over the grief; I got *into* it fully. This emboldened me to document the childhood scars as fiercely as I endured them. After all, the clarion call of "Famine" demanded that I tell the unadulterated truth. In going deep in the pain, a light was sure enough coming through. I understood what writer Paula D'Arcy meant when she wrote in *Stars at Night: When Darkness Unfolds as Light*, "An apprenticeship with the night is an inheritance I would wish for everyone."

4. Forgive

To be candid, forgiveness wasn't so hard for me. I know that's a "don't hate me because I'm beautiful" type of statement, and I hope you'll humor me.

Through an inexplicable grace, I'd largely absolved the perpetrators in my story. But there were lingering pockets of poison in me, and the wound would require the debridement of forgiveness.

Eventually I got there—again by the therapeutic practice of writing through it with balls-to-the-wall honesty—just as Sinéad modeled in "Famine." This is when I could hear the chains of generational depravity shattering. Strongholds giving way. I was free now.

Had I held on to the grudges and blame and hurts, the memoir would have read as a revenge play. Instead, I pray it's a realistic tale of posttraumatic growth.

While I plugged along with the writing, my family begged me not to tell the story. A melodramatic sister—reminding me that Mama's nerves were already shot—predicted this would be the final nail in her coffin.

An aunt denounced the venture as pointless and unseemly. The choir of others couldn't comprehend why I'd create something that would inflict more damage. *Don't air the dirty laundry. Keep quiet. You might not have a family left if you do this.*

As Sinéad says in her memoir, *Rememberings*, "Some things are worth being a pariah for."

Once my book was with the publisher—and not a word could be changed—I sent Mama the manuscript. I was scared shitless. Would she shun me? Would she wage war in defense of the fantasies she'd concocted? Or might she actually accept what I'd written?

Mama took the manuscript to her bathroom so that she could read it in private. Her longtime live-in partner knew only her version of things, so she needed to see what I'd revealed. As the sun rose the following morning, she emerged from the bathroom and handed him the manuscript.

"Here's Retta's book," she said. "Every bit of it is the truth, and I don't give a damn what you think of it."

Releasing the story liberated her as well.

Obviously, I stumbled onto rich spiritual terrain in the process of crafting the memoir. I suspect it's because truth-speaking is inherently sacred. Writing is soul work. Unmasking lies and liars is a form of spiritual warfare that carries grave danger. In this regard, Sinéad was a supreme combatant.

Like Scáthach, the noted female warrior of Celtic mythology, she was also a teacher of warriors. Scáthach's students owed their prowess to her training, and she equipped them with weapons of her own invention, one of which was a barbed harpoon.

Clearly, Sinéad heaved such a harpoon when she tore up the photo of Pope John Paul II. Despite the backlash it unleashed, it achieved her mission to lay bare the child sexual abuse in the Roman Catholic Church.

"My own dream is only to keep the contract I made with God before I ever made one with the music business," she says in *Rememberings*.

Later she adds, "I'm certain part of the reason I became a singer was that I couldn't become a priest, given that I had a vagina and a pair of breasts (however insignificant)."

In "Famine," Sinéad advocates the worship of God as a mother, as was the old practice in Ireland. She believes a Feminine Divinity will help in the healing.

At the time I was writing my book, my spirituality consisted of a free-form, hodgepodge belief system. Yet "Famine" ultimately provided transformative direction that drew me closer to God.

Much to everyone's shock and to some folks' horror, a decade later I'd become a Roman Catholic with a singular devotion to Mary, Mother of God.

I realize the Church would tremble in its cassocks at the following thought, but I'm convinced Sinéad O'Connor was a saint, however dissident. Sound ridiculous?

Consider the lives saved through the intercession of her lamentations, lullabies, anthems, and war cries. Their testimonies flooded social media upon word of her death. Listeners attest that prayers and petitions were heard and answered through her music. Her songs are numinous and liminal, thresholds and thin places.

Like St. Teresa of Ávila and St. Francis of Assisi, she brought about purifying reform in the Church. Once she shredded the Holy Father's photo in front of millions of viewers, the jig was up. The Church had to respond and disinfect.

As it turns out, "Famine" certainly did have something for me, something far surpassing what I could discern during that first listen. And Sinéad continues to abide in the innermost hidden place of my creative and spiritual aspirations.

Eight months after a publisher bought my memoir, *The Cracker Queen,* I watched her perform at a concert hall in Atlanta, Georgia. To no one's surprise, she blew the roof off the mutha. The venue, which had formerly been a church, was appropriately named the Tabernacle.

"I've done only one holy thing in my life and that was sing," says Sinéad in *Rememberings*.

Beloved badass saint, it was more than enough.

Sunshower

"The Wolf Is Getting Married"

MARTHA BAYNE

For years the hardest song in the book to sing, for me, was a love song. Songs of anger, of longing, of regret or despair—those were easy. Even songs of good fun, shot through with irony and wit, those were okay, too. But a love song? I don't know. So corny. So unrealistic, really. I didn't need that.

It wasn't always this way. As a girl I sang from the same songbook as everybody else, Captain and Tennille, Stevie Wonder, and the Bee Gees charting the map of adult love. My sisters and I put on shows in the basement, lip-syncing to the *Grease* cast recording, "You're the One That I Want" transgressive with its asked-and-answered expression of Sandy's desire, problematic makeover notwithstanding.

In high school I entered into the post-punk underground of 1980s Seattle, a thrilling place to be. Around every corner boys with guitars howled and groaned, and the girls watched as their grinding efforts were rewarded with acclaim. We longed to be them, or be close to them, and it was often unclear where the distinction lay. But Green River didn't write love songs. Ironic distance was the posture of the day, and we learned early on that sentiment had no place in the scene.

Or I did, at least, and I assumed I was just following commonly understood rules: be cool, act chill. We were young and it was special, this moment, so don't try too hard, want anything, get in the way.

Wanting a boyfriend was decidedly uncool, I perceived. So when I had a crush on the cute boy who hung out at the espresso bar downtown, my friends and I just taunted him on the bus with a loud rendition of "You're So Vain." But despite such bravado, somehow both genuine and a front, I did want . . . something. I just couldn't find the agency to name it in the bright light of day.

Instead, teenage sex was fleeting, muddied in the slippery borderlands of consent. Does it even matter? I don't know anymore, whatever early trauma it caused so baked into my bones that to deny the damage would be to cut off an arm. But back then I told myself it didn't matter when the soccer jock fucked me on the beach and harassed me in the halls. It didn't matter when the manager talked me into a blowjob at the party with the band. It didn't matter that the new boy, who I really liked, kicked me out of bed when he was done. He had places to be that held more promise than me, as the 1980s held such promise for scruffy young men in Seattle, and I accepted this, like smoking, as the price of admittance to adulthood, a land I was eager to explore.

My first real boyfriend, at eighteen, won me by cutting against the grain. He lit candles and hung tapestries, bought bottles of cheap wine instead of half-racks of Oly. He played along to "Avalon" on his guitar, crooning his best Bryan Ferry. I found it intoxicating, if suspect—and when he developed a drug problem and started sleeping with his roommate I told myself that didn't matter, either, not at all.

By then I was in the Midwest, in college, where I told myself it didn't matter that I had left this sordid catalog of adolescent insults behind.

In college I fell in love—twice! And Sinéad O'Connor, singing about love and pain and desire, surfaced through the din of college radio to share space with Kim Gordon and Ann Magnuson, these iterations of incantatory, fearless women replacing shaggy-haired boys as the poles of mid-'80s cool against which I took my measure.

Neither of my college loves lasted, but they were sweet. And as I pushed forward into adulthood I believed them the foundation of an inevitable arc toward mature love. I'd started out rocky, sure—didn't everyone? But I'd found my footing, I was growing into agency, exploring and experimenting, to better and worse ends. By the time I was thirty I found my boyfriend's full-throated renditions of Jeff Buckley ballads endearing in their searching, earnest passion, where once I might have cringed. That relationship didn't last either but at least, I told myself, I was listening.

Then, the needle skittered off the record in a hit and run of sexual violence so empty of meaning I can only liken it to an encounter with a bear. I was attacked by a bear, I came to tell myself, and for the ten years that followed, as if in a fairy tale, I became a wolf.

As a wolf, I was no noble predator, big and bad, nor one with which a woman might want to run. I felt lone, a scavenger, scratching for intimacy and nourishment in the dark corners of after-hours bars and other women's men. I told myself it didn't matter, that I lacked for nothing I didn't desire. And besides, it might have been my fault, the violation I couldn't forget, the secret I couldn't share. You're supposed to fight back against the threat of certain bears, make yourself large and loud. But you should make yourself small in the face of others, say the survival guides. Stay quiet; don't look them in the eye. In my drunkenness and confusion, had I frozen when I should have screamed?

At the time my friends were settling down, having babies. I didn't want to scare them, so I worked hard to hide my wolfishness from the world, kept my matted fur and gnawing hunger under wraps. And, like the wolf in grandma's bonnet I succeeded, and even thrived, in sideways fashion. It didn't matter that in my feral panic I'd left the job that kept me grounded, flush, and credible. I chose this, I insisted. I'm better off this way. I could barely pay the rent but I'd rather be foraging in the freelance woods, wouldn't you?

Really, I was so ashamed I couldn't begin to let anyone in to witness the truth of my life. I don't remember much music at all.

In 2012 I was forty-four and living with a friend in my one-bedroom apartment. We slept in shifts, like flight attendants, or med students, him on the couch until I went to work my day shift on the copy desk, then moving to the bedroom to take over the still-warm bed. Secretly, I sort of liked this arrangement, though I knew it was unbecoming and often felt judged. A roommate? At my age? But I liked the company, and the odd domestic cosplay. Maybe, I wondered, there was something I did want?

That same year I got pregnant by accident, and had a miscarriage, and in the brief window between those two events realized this was something I maybe did want as well. I wrote an essay about these events that went viral, to the point that I was invited onto *Fresh Air* to talk with Terry Gross. But in the studio I choked, frozen in fear of exposing the ugly animal of my sex life to the NPR listening audience. The segment never aired, for which I remain grateful.

And that same year Sinéad O'Connor, one year older than me, released her ninth album, *How About I Be Me (and You Be You)?* After the back-to-back successes of *The Lion and the Cobra* and *I Do Not Want What I Haven't Got* rocketed her to stardom and her 1992 *Saturday Night Live* appearance crashed that rocket into the sun, she had retreated, retrenched. She released an album of standards, a reggae album, an album of Celtic folk. She was ordained a priest in a splinter sect of the Catholic Church, was diagnosed as bipolar, came out as a lesbian, then turned around and married a man, her fourth, and then split from him, and reconciled within a month. And then she released this album, widely hailed as a triumphant return to form, an album dominated by, of all things, love songs.

On the jaunty "4th and Vine," she sings about putting her pink dress on and going down to the church where she's "gonna marry my love/and we'll be happy for all time." In "Old Lady," she sings of a man for whom, in the present, she fronts as too cool to care for, but in the future, she fantasizes, when "I'm an old lady/I'm gonna be his baby." And "I Had a Baby" is a love song to just that: a baby, one whose origins in "a fling with/A man who wasn't mine to be with" painfully mirror those of the baby of mine that never was.

If I heard this album in 2012, I don't remember. I wish I did, but in truth, at the time O'Connor had fallen off my radar, as she had for so many. But in the months and years that followed the miscarriage, my roommate and I moved to an apartment with two bedrooms, I found a new job I loved, and I started to build a new narrative, inscribed in large part through a reclamation of autonomy over my body and a pursuit of physical strength that continues to this day.

Ten years later, on the cusp of my own wedding, I was poking around online for "songs about marriage," making a playlist for the party, and there it was, *How About*'s first single, "The Wolf Is Getting Married." The title came, O'Connor once told reporters, from a conversation with a London cabbie. It's an Arab expression used to refer to a patch of blue on a cloudy day, a variant of a common global idiom for the phenomenon of a sunshower, rain falling while the sun is shining. Full-throated and unapologetic—no too-cool-for-school posing, no secrets, no shame—the song soars on her clarion voice, a love song charting a character who once had "no safety . . . no solid foundation to keep me."

Sinéad O'Connor, who had been married four times, who had been abused by her mother, who had been betrayed by the Church and by the music industry in turn, who had an abortion, several miscarriages, and four babies, and whose breakdown in early 2012 prevented her from fully touring in support of this comeback album, declares:

Your smile makes me smile
Your laugh makes me laugh
Your joy gives me joy
Your hope gives me hope

Struck by this optimistic expression of belief in the transformative power of love, arresting in its purity, I listened, emotion choking my chest the way it did when I finally told someone about the bear.

She sang:

Even when something terrible is happening
you laugh and that's the thing I love about you most.

When I first started seeing the man who became my husband, during the first summer of the Covid pandemic, we engaged in an extended debate, alternately agonizing and comic, about the possibility of physical contact and the potential exchange of bodily fluids. I like to think that this ridiculous exploration of consent laid the foundation for the durability of our bond.

We got married two years later in a Wisconsin park, on a day that started and ended with rain, but whose skies cleared to pure blue in between. We walked down the aisle to the Monkees' "You Just May Be the One," the goofiest of love songs, played on guitar and accordion. I wasn't expecting this happy, heteronormative twist to the dark fairy tale of the past and, indeed, I was diagnosed with breast cancer just days before the wedding, a story for another time. But upon meeting my husband it had quickly become clear that it was still possible for the sun to again peek out from a long-gray sky.

We don't have to be defined by trauma, but we must make peace with the strange shape into which its impact has pressed our lives before we can open up the songbook with joy and sing with the open-hearted glee of a wolf howling at the altar.

Holy Shit (A Love Letter)

"Song to the Siren"

LIDIA YUKNAVITCH

2010

I am forty-seven, drinking a Guinness in a Portland bar with my third husband. He is talking to me about the film he wants to make and I am in love with listening. Specifically, I love listening to anyone talk about the art they want to make. I believe in art the way other people believe in God, which is a line I've tried to sneak into almost everything I've ever written. The line is both my fuck-you to organized religion as a recovering Catholic, as well as my puny attempt to raise a fist to those who would silence artists. Or maybe it's my version of a secular prayer.

I'm listening to what he is saying to me with great focus, up until I hear a voice penetrating the bar din. I sip my Guinness. I recognize the voice. Sinéad O'Connor's voice weaves its way into my skull. Something between a wail and a lullaby, if lullabies could perform sweet and scream at the same time. I mean, that voice could penetrate any din. Like a Siren luring the listener in. The more Sinéad sings, the more Sinéad the song becomes. Sinéad O'Connor's voice makes interrupting my beautiful husband's art-mouth worth it.

I put my finger to my lips and say *shhhhhhhhh*. Listen, I say. I point to my own ear and then to the air like that's a clear communication.

My third husband hushes and listens.

I close my eyes.

Holy shit, I say in the air between us. This is like my favorite song of all time, I say. A dumb sentence carrying decades of my life in it.

He listens. Oh—"Song to the Siren," right? This Mortal Coil?

Yeah, I say. But this is Sinéad O'Connor. Just . . . her voice . . . *holy shit.*

He listens for a few beats. Yeah, he says. Amazing. Is she okay? I heard she became a priest?

But I'm lost in the listening, somewhere between *holy shit* and her voice recovering my whole life.

1992

I am twenty-nine, drinking a Guinness with my second husband in our living room. We are watching *SNL* the night Sinéad O'Connor rips up the pope photo. *Holy shit,* he says. I sit there both mesmerized by her hands and face, as well as impressed with how perfect the phrase *holy shit* fits the moment. Then I have a jolting flashback.

I flash back to being ten years old. Back to my father's violence in my childhood home. I flash back to the Catholic CCD classes with their strange and deformed mix of violence and the seduction of children. I flash back to my own acts of truancy, theft, breaking-and-entering, kid crimes that would bloom into real crimes later in life. I flash back to lying in the confessional booth. I flash back to stealing money from the collection plates, also the coat pockets of people in the congregation.

My tenth year was the year my sister went to college and never returned. Put simply, she fled to save her own life. Her survival strategy was to disassociate and bury herself inward during her childhood and adolescence. Her portal was a life of the mind. My sister was and is brilliant. My sister was and is an artist, poet, educator, and healer.

My sister and I were both raised Catholic. She chose Joan as her confirmation name, from St. Joan of Arc, which impressed me mightily as a child. Catholicism did not work on me. When I was ten my Catechism breached. I tried to stab the hand of a nun with a just-sharpened pencil. She'd raised her hand to a friend of mine like she was going to slap her in the face. I watched the nun's hand in the air, like the breath before a blow. If I'd made it to Confirmation, I would have chosen the name Muhammad Ali, or Bruce Lee, two of my favorite humans on the planet. Both fighters. Alas, neither were saints, and I didn't make it to Confirmation anyway. Consequently I have no middle name, just a space which waited for me like a breath between my first name—chosen by my father—and my last name, one I'd leave forever when I got the chance.

A schism opened up when my sister left. Another way to say this is when I turned ten, and my father's eyes and hands turned toward me, I had to learn how to defend myself from violence and transgression. Had I not learned this lesson quickly, I would have spent the next eight years being tortured. Instead, I just spent them receiving and transforming abuse while simultaneously becoming physically strong as a competitive swimmer. The words *father* and *family* and the word *home* have always felt vaguely carceral to me. I saw correlates in the world outside of my home everywhere. My survival strategy thus formed into a kind of tough-bodied strength, that of the fighter. My portal was rage. I wanted to rip the world to shreds.

Raging your way through life has deep costs. I mean sure, you can fight your way out of tricky situations or transgressions, you can even fight for others, but what are you fighting your way *into*? Or where does the rage go when need drives the fist of you? I became a kind of avenging angel in life, but without the skills to understand or channel that might, I nearly self-immolated. Many times. For this reason, I have no problem understanding people who self-destruct. I'm not even sure I'd call it self-destruction. More like . . . rage that gets lost looking for a form to hold it. I've noticed rage and the ability to fight, when it shows up in the body of a woman, receives condemnation and punishment more often than not.

I flash forward again to the present tense, where a pope on a piece of paper has been ripped up by a brave, brilliant young woman artist with a shaved head. Perfect avenging angel for all of us children who have suffered child sexual abuse at the hands of the fathers.

Rip the photo to shreds. Rip the images into pieces, burn the pieces, eat the pieces, drown the pieces in Communion water. Sinéad O'Connor, Joan of Arc. Hail Sinéad, full of the grace of grit. Save us from all the fathers and mothers who betray children.

That was incredible, I say to my second husband, into the silence after the televised moment. I leave my past where it belongs, but something in me is singing, or is it screaming? My bones are ringing like tuning forks. I think about artists who take risks and artists who do not.

Holy shit, my second husband says, stretching the moment out as if hope—the hope of a painter and a writer making for the world—might have a voice between us, many years before he will die by suicide.

1983

I am twenty. My baby girl has died on the day of her birth. I could fill pages and pages with that story, and I have, but what I want to say right now carries the brevity of breath.

I want to go to death by water, as she lived and died in the waters of my belly. I take her ashes to the Pacific Ocean. I walk into the water to disperse her, but I keep walking. I want to follow her. Into the water. Forever. I can't imagine living without her. I want to be enfolded by the water.

My first husband, father of my dead baby girl, wades out into the ocean to retrieve me. My first husband has the longest most delicate fingers in the world. I let him guide me back to shore. My long wool coat is bright red. In the sea water it pulls downward with weight. I am between worlds.

My choice would have been to lose myself to the water with my dead baby girl. There is no language capable of holding this feeling.

In the moment, in the water, his choice wins, therefore, I live.

My first husband, the virtuoso guitar player, the masterful artist, painter, covers me in warm blankets back at home. He feeds me soup with a spoon. I'm like a newborn. He puts earphones on my useless skull.

In my ears is a song I have never heard before. The song floods my body. Later he will tell me it is "Song to the Siren." This version of the Tim Buckley original is covered by Elizabeth Fraser from This Mortal Coil. Her voice sounds like a song underwater, echoing. She sings open a space between life and death. She sounds like the Siren she sings of.

The song makes me heave oceans. But the lyrics are everything of what I am feeling. Death. Love. Swim to me let me enfold you. Here I am. Waiting to hold you. I listen to the song over and over again. I am wailing. My eyes are so puffed up I can't see. Snot everywhere. Grief drool. But I am smiling—a kind of snarl or scream-smile—and nodding my head yes. *Holy shit,* I whisper. How music reverbs over time and space, comes to you differently at different times in your life. How art can save your life inside death, or maybe carry you home when you are ready, however you might travel.

Precious to Me

"My Special Child"

JILL CHRISTMAN

On a dark stage in Düsseldorf in 1990, Sinéad O'Connor puts down her guitar and picks up a plastic cup containing what looks like a cider slushy. Stirring the thick drink with a spoon and looking shy, she says, "I'm actually going to do a new song. It's called 'My Special Child.'"

The audience screams, lighters sway along with the bootlegger's camera. Sinéad's been shedding clothes throughout the show and now she's wearing faded jeans, a thick black belt, a black bra, black boots. This will be the last song of the first concert on this tour. She paces circles, readying her body for what comes next as the opening note swells—but then someone throws something onto the stage, something big.

Sinéad smiles. Sinéad *giggles*. Face shining with delight, she puts her hand to her heart, then turns to the band and waves them to stop. "All right," she says into the mic. "Who threw that?" She walks to the edge of the stage and hoists a huge stuffed rabbit by its baby blue ears, reading the attached note and saying, "Awwww." Sinéad carries the rabbit to the back and plumps him into position under the drum kit, makes sure he's sitting up straight to enjoy the show. The strings begin again.

If my mother ever talked to me about abortion, I don't remember. The first I witnessed up close was an abortion chosen by an intimate college friend—we'll call her K—and K must have had about as much real education in this arena as me. She had unprotected sex on Memorial Day weekend in 1988 and then went home to another state for the whole summer. We were both just turning nineteen and K couldn't have weighed more than 115 pounds soaking wet. When she returned in August, she was wearing a huge T-shirt to disguise the situation, but when she lifted it, she had her tight jeans hooked with a safety pin and her stomach pushed over the top.

"I think," she began. We both stared at her belly as if we were expecting it to talk. "Do you think?" she began again.

I moved my eyes from K's belly to her eyes.

"I think I might be pregnant," she said.

She told me she'd been partying all summer, that she was afraid. She had a million other theories that could explain her growing belly and disappeared period. Somehow we got our hands on a drugstore pregnancy test and confirmed what K didn't want to know.

K was too terrified to tell *her* parents. We told my mom, who told her boyfriend, who apparently had some experience in these matters. I realize now that K must have been at least fourteen weeks pregnant, so the abortion was scheduled quickly. K was forced to tell her parents after all because of money. Her dad came to town with his stricken face and checkbook, and K endured what I remember as a two-day ordeal. We don't stay in touch, but just once, twenty years later, K made contact and told me about her daughter, her heart, the child she was ready for. The child she chose.

How to do justice to Sinéad O'Connor? It feels impossible, like writing something for a teacher who has challenged you, the one you love and respect above all others. To say that thing we all say—"We did not deserve her"—is certainly true, but not even close to enough.

Sinéad was three years older than me. She was a Doc-Martens-wearing punk from Dublin and I was a peasant-skirt-crop-top-wearing hippie from the mountains of Washington State, but we shared some fundamental knowledge of the world's wounding. In the five years between 1987 and 1992, I made it through college at the University of Oregon with a year off to wander Central America with a notebook, grieving my fiancé who died in a car accident during my sophomore year and working hard to heal from years of childhood sexual abuse and a fraternity-party rape. In 1987 Sinéad gave birth to her first son, Jake, and then, three weeks later, launched her debut album. She released *I Do Not Want What I Haven't Got* in 1990, an album her Ensign producer Nigel Grainge wanted to scratch because it was "too personal." As Sinéad writes in *Rememberings*: "[Nigel] is such an (oxy)moron. How can a song be too personal? I imagined slapping him lightly about the temples with a large raw fish. That's the only thing to do with stupid people."

That second album came out as I navigated a return to life with my new knowledge of death and my determination to survive, those "too personal" songs coding themselves into the wounds and folds of my still-elastic brain with the permanence that only repeat, whole-album listening during a time of deep need brings us. Sinéad said in interviews that Bob Dylan's *Slow Train Coming* became a surrogate father after her parents' divorce when she was forced to live with her abusive mother. "Gotta Serve Somebody," in particular, guided Sinéad to understand that she wanted to be a musician and what *kind* of musician she wanted to be. Sinéad was nearly my contemporary, but her music mothered me. I determined I would write stories, stories from my life, and those stories would be as personal as they needed to be.

Sinéad gave me space to weep and scream and rip shit up. Sinéad told the truth about things that people in my actual life did not—about child abuse, the policing of women's bodies, misogyny, and injustice wherever and whenever she saw it happening. Her voice and music came into my life when I needed to talk about living in a body that had been misused, a body that still wasn't safe—not in the streets, not on my own campus, not in our courts. She started those conversations as if they were normal, even under the most *abnormal* of circumstances in the hot-white early years of her career: "I was just being a punk. That's what punks do."

Sinéad was willing to look at her own pain and to bring that pain into the light, which helped her to see the whole world clearly. She wanted us to be frightened of the right things, like child abuse, not the wrong things—music, say, or a twenty-four-year-old musician tearing up a photograph. In *Rememberings,* Sinéad recounts the hours after her *SNL* appearance, back in her hotel room: "The matter is being discussed on the news and we learn I am banned from NBC for life. This hurts me a lot less than rapes hurt those Irish children."

After K's abortion, I paid closer attention, and art came through. Lucille Clifton and Ani DiFranco and Sinéad O'Connor taught me about abortion after all other sex education had failed me.

Sinéad released *My Special Child* in 1991 as a seven-inch with four songs: the brand-new song, an instrumental, and live recordings of both "Nothing Compares 2 U" and "Emperor's New Clothes" with all proceeds benefiting the International Red Cross Kurdish Relief Program to raise awareness of child abuse. If you were around in 1991, you were most likely to find the song through the video on MTV—as I did.

"My Special Child" begins with a light falling from the sky and a sustained note that hits my ear like an echo of the first seven seconds of "Nothing Compares 2 U." But as the Irish bagpipes rise, we see Sinéad's hands plucking petals off white blossoms, the froth of a waterfall, and then her bright eyes veiled by the mist. A child's sneakered feet kick a clear glass marble the size of a tangerine. In a bare white room Sinéad sits on the floor dressed in white meditation clothes, her shoulder to the wall, gazing toward the square window, the smoke of the incense rising in hazy ribbons around her head. The shot widens to include the child—a boy in a white sailor suit—and the domestic folds with the spiritual like bed sheets.

She begins singing and we see her face in close-up, eyes outlined in smoky black, "Nothing Compares 2 U"–style, with the same clarity of gaze and annunciation that pins us in place:

Think about my little girl
Her yellow skin and her dark curls
And how her father's heart was frozen

In her expression: grief and betrayal, fury and love. The white curtain billows and the boy rolls around playfully on the white-sheeted mattress pushed against the opposite wall. Sinéad lies on the mattress with her shirt pulled up, hands on her belly. A pregnancy remembered and honored.

I spoke to her and I said:
"You won't regret the mother you have chosen."
I lied.
Where is she tonight?

"My Special Child" is about an abortion Sinéad had in 1990—a mournful love song to a lost child that also channels her anger and considers all the choices: her own to end the pregnancy even though it "had been planned, and [she] was madly in love with the father of the child," the father who "wasn't going to be around," and even the child who has "chosen" these parents.

She could not have gotten an abortion in Ireland that year, so she would have traveled outside of her own country to seek care—this trip to England was so common it was called "the Irish Journey." At a pro-choice rally in Dublin in 1992, Sinéad's hands shook as she stood at the mic: "If you're going to admit that a girl who has been raped should be allowed to leave the country to have an abortion, then why not admit she should be allowed to have it here? . . . to send her away to another country is an Irish solution to an Irish problem."

In the video, Sinéad reappears in a yellow flowered dress, holding the glass sphere up to the light of the window as if she's using it to see her child in another realm. Cut to sky and clouds—a shot of heaven. Once I get the idea of scrying in my head, it's everywhere—looking into, looking through light and shadow and smoke and a tiny crystal ball. It reminds me of the gorgeous way Sinéad describes getting confirmation of her pregnancy with her first child, Jake: "Had to pee in a tiny glass tube that had a small globule of light yellow jelly inside and then sit the tube in a little holder that had a small mirror underneath in which soon a lovely pink circle appeared. Beautiful-looking thing it was too, like a little planet."

Sinéad is talking to her baby in that sphere—and she is talking about choice. She has made her decision, the pregnancy is ended, but as she told *Spin* in 1991, no abortion is easy:

> So I was very distraught; it wasn't a decision that I made lightly, or that anyone makes lightly. It took me a year to get over it, but it was the right decision. I just believe that if a child is meant to be born it will be born. It doesn't really matter whether you have an abortion or a miscarriage. The whole issue is pro-choice.

"My Special Child" traces Sinéad's decision and experience—as a mother, a deeply spiritual person, and a musician. Every choice to end a pregnancy is made by an individual in a particular set of circumstances in a singular moment. The diversity of our experience makes it impossible for anyone else to make that decision or conjecture about what we would have done. We do not know. We *cannot* know. Sinéad was twenty-one and in the studio for her first album with Ensign when that first little pink planet appeared in the test tube. She felt elation. Pure joy. She felt ready to be this child's mother. Her record label felt differently. In *Rememberings,* Sinéad reports:

> The doctor told me Nigel had already called him and expressed the wish that he, the doctor, would impress upon me the following, which he, the doctor, said in the following words, "Your record company has spent a hundred thousand pounds recording your album. You owe it to them not to have this baby."

As Sinéad knew from the first glow of that tiny affirming pink planet in the bottom of the test tube, reproductive rights—and the lack of them—are not, nor have they ever been, about the lives of babies (or, God forbid, women), but about the controlling of women. In this case, a lot of men had a lot of money to lose—so they wanted Sinéad to have an abortion. Sinéad didn't care what her record company thought about her pregnancy and Jake was born.

"My Special Child" has no chorus; the song is constructed from four verses that build in tempo and volume, and in the middle, a shift, a spoken address to the aborted child. In the video, she speaks to the crystal ball: "You were precious to me." And then everything turns to Jake. He puts down the Tibetan prayer wheel he's been spinning and pulls open the wooden door to a sunny day. The tempo builds, Sinéad sings "don't cry, everything's all right," and the shots alternate between mother and son hugging and playing in the sand. Everything feels bright and good.

In the closing shot, Sinéad and Jake cuddle close on the white bed, backs to the wall, looking at a photo album together. On the last page, the photo we get to see: a white horse sitting like a dog. In Christianity, the white horse is a symbol of death, but in Irish mythology, that same horse represents fertility and purity. This collision of interpretation doesn't surprise me, and in fact, feels precisely Sinéad: let that white horse be both life and death. But the sitting? The sitting is weird. Horses rarely sit. Maybe Jake knows? In the final frame, Jake says something into Sinéad's ear—and she is listening carefully.

Processing trauma through music, Sinéad insisted on being all the parts of herself—enraged, joyful, sexual, spiritual, funny, flawed, maternal, fierce, vulnerable—and showed me that I could do the same.

I've never had an unwanted pregnancy, but when I was thirty-seven years old and nineteen weeks pregnant with a much-wanted baby boy, a routine ultrasound revealed he had only half a heart. The pediatric cardiologist in Indianapolis told us that our baby's condition was "incompatible with life" and gave us two official options: palliative care or a three-stage surgery that had, as of 2006, carried some of the longest surviving "blue babies" into their teen years with replumbed half hearts. The cardiologist also gave us a third, hushed option—"termination"—reminding us that his was "a Catholic hospital" and we'd have to seek consultation elsewhere.

I'd be lying if I told you I thought of Sinéad in the four nightmarish days that passed between our baby's diagnosis and the second trimester abortion that ended my pregnancy in Chicago, three hundred miles from our home. Over the phone, provider after provider in my home state told me it was too late, there was nothing they could do, or—the worst—they did have one doctor who would perform the abortion in Indianapolis, but I had to bring cash and "some Tylenol for after the procedure." I might, the receptionist said, have "some discomfort." Are you *shitting* me? As someone who has been through the operation, I want to say that to perform a dilation and extraction without general anesthesia is physically brutal and emotionally cruel. The idea was that I did not deserve to be treated with care—and this was 2006. *Roe* v. *Wade* was still the law of the land and abortion in Indiana was legal up to twenty-two weeks. Three years earlier, I'd hemorrhaged after our daughter's birth; if I hadn't been in a hospital, I would have died. I never want to hear *I would have done this* or *I would have done that*. The air hunger, the bleeding, the preschooler waiting at home: nobody knows what choice they would make until they are there, exactly there. Until they are in it.

So, no, I wasn't thinking about Sinéad in the blur of those dark days, but through her voice she had taught me about my own value, about choice, about the way one chosen abortion might make a path for the next chosen special child.

Back in 1990 Düsseldorf in that bootleg video, Sinéad sings "My Special Child" in a luminous, bell-like voice, and then a whisper. She sings with her whole body, bringing her arms forward as if she's offering her unborn child a gift, her message so clear when she speaks: "*You were precious to me / After all I called you into being / I wanted you to know that.*" It's as if she's saying goodbye. Then she returns to the world of the song where Jake is waiting, her arms a cradle, patting the air with urgent, joyful hands, her final words on the Düsseldorf stage: "Don't cry. Jake's here tonight."

Sinéad turns away from the mic and heads straight for the rabbit, lifting him by his generous ears and slipping through a gap in the dark curtain.

Maybe Jake is back there. Maybe she is bringing him the rabbit.

Sorry for Disappointing

"Daddy I'm Fine"

RAYNE FISHER-QUANN

The day that Sinéad died, my father cried alone in a bar in Quebec. I know this because he texted me about it, said the French-Canadian bartender didn't understand at all when he tried to explain why, and then sent me a link to the song "Daddy I'm Fine." "This song always reminded me of you and your sibling," he said. I could tell that he was still crying. And then, five minutes later, a follow-up text: "To be clear, there are some lyrics in that song i absolutely DO NOT associate with you."

He had to say that, of course, in the name of fatherly couth—there are a lot of lyrics in the song about pushing your boobs up and wanting to fuck every man in sight and so on and so forth. But the beauty of the song, the source of its triumph but also its hidden complexity, is that it's all much more about *wanting* than it is *doing*. She isn't singing about actually being promiscuous, per se (at least not yet); she's singing about how badly she wants to be able to *act* like she is. She sings about wanting to feel sexy under the lights, to slick back her hair, to dress like the kind of woman who might implore a guy at the bar to come home with her. It's a song about the part of your life where the whole world stretches out before you, perilous but wide, and you're stuck with the beauty and the terror of trying to choose what kind of person you might be once you're in it.

It's also a song about dropping out of school and leaving your hometown to be an artist in a big city, which is precisely what happened to me in the years before my father texted me from the bar in Quebec, so it's not surprising that he thinks of me when he listens to it—he who has been on the receiving end of countless long-distance phone calls in which I probably whined the words "Daddy, I'm fine" verbatim. But even with all of its technical relatabilities, the crux of my connection to the song is much more about the former feeling, the one that's harder to pin down: the feeling of aching for a new world, aching to be a different kind of person, wondering if it's possible to try on the trappings of a life before you're ready for it and turn into the person you want to be along the way. I've never exactly wanted to fuck a random guy at the bar, but I want, almost constantly, to know what it must be like to be the kind of woman who would.

Faith and Courage came out a year before I was born, and my mother, a devoutly feminist ex-Catholic who left her hometown in her late teens and the Church when I was a baby, listened to it with religious fervor throughout my childhood. The text from my father was a reintroduction that came at a serendipitous time: it was days after a breakup with my long-term boyfriend, a good man from my hometown who I loved dearly, who I lived with, who gave me a comfortable life, and who I left because I felt in my stomach that I had to be by myself in a place I'd never been before or my life might be for nothing. It was one of those rare and precious moments where a work of art reveals itself to you at precisely the time you need it most. In the months that followed, I listened to "Daddy I'm Fine" on loop, nonstop, on the plane to LaGuardia, as I went to sign my first solo lease, on my walks home from parties full of strangers. I'm fine, I'm fine, I'm fine.

But as good as it feels to relate to a song like this one, relatability can be a kind of trap. Good art helps you understand yourself, and great art feels like it becomes a part of who you are, and both of those experiences create deep, real intimacy without proximity—without real knowledge of the person on the other side of the transaction. When art and its artist feel like they are speaking not just to you but in some way *from* you, it's easy to feel like they belong to you; like their words, and by extension their life, are just as much yours as they are theirs. But Sinéad, perhaps more than anyone, belonged to no one. And so I keep having to remind myself that I don't really know Sinéad. To try to write about someone else's art just by consuming it is a bit like trying to draw someone else by looking at them through a two-way mirror: the result will always look at least a little like you.

Like Sinéad herself, "Daddy I'm Fine" is full of contradiction. It's a song written in part from the perspective of a person in the distant past, and as a result, we're given a kind of contextual omnipotence over the version of Sinéad whose story we're hearing—we listen to it knowing what happened to her after she moved to London, about her struggles with fame, about her well-documented pain. Part of the magic of the song, in fact, is that what it celebrates is not a straightforward victory. We know from songs like "Black Boys on Mopeds" that Sinéad was not fond of England and had no easy feelings about living there, even as she describes London as a kind of escape from the oppression of home. She had a complicated relationship with her own sexuality, with being sexualized, with relationships with men in general. She said in a 2000 interview that she wished she'd dressed sexier in her twenties, implying that she didn't quite embody the fantasy that she sings about wanting at the time. Even her dream of making a living through music, a dream she accomplished, was complicated by constant clashes with her record label as they tried to manufacture her into a consumable pop star. These aren't flaws in the song, or in her life; they're the whole point. Those complexities are what elevate "Daddy I'm Fine" beyond the class of straightforward girl-power anthems and into something much more nuanced, more interesting, at once both sadder and much more hopeful. It's a song, simply put, about faith and courage. If life was simple, what would be the use of either?

I'm reminded of a quote by Jacqueline Rose, writing about Marilyn Monroe in her book *Women in Dark Times*: "I do not find it helpful to present her—or indeed any woman—as either on top of or succumbing to her demons, as though her only options were victory or defeat (a military vocabulary which could not be further from her own)." The song is not a celebration of victory so much as it is a celebration of freedom, a chasmic difference that you can only truly understand once you've had to make a choice between the two.

"Daddy I'm Fine" is, of course, a song about fathers, but as with all Sinéad songs, I can't help but think of my mother when I listen to it. And I can't think of my mother without thinking of her mother—another woman, like all women in my maternal lineage, whose daughter left her in search of a different life.

My granny was a prototypical Irish Catholic: tough, blunt, honest, needing no comfort, wanting no frivolity. I wonder, often, what she would think of the type of woman I grew into—emotional, expressive to a fault, thin-skinned, definitionally frivolous. I sensed her disapproval of me even when I was a teenager; when I wore ripped jeans, when I wouldn't do the dishes. I loved her, and I know for certain that she loved me intensely, but it often felt like a ritual kind of love, instinctual, rather than a love born of anything we actually had in common. I didn't think that she understood me, and I don't think I tried very hard to understand her.

Years after my granny died, though, my mother mentioned offhandedly in conversation that she had denied my grandfather's marriage proposal three times before finally accepting, even though marriage to a good man, a man that she loved desperately until the day she died, was just about all that a woman could be expected to aspire to in the 1950s. I felt like the air had been knocked out of me, which is how I still feel now whenever I think about her—how little I knew of her, how much there was to understand. I realized with the shame of a child that I'd had it all wrong.

She, too, had an instinctive resistance to the life that had been set out for her; perhaps she, too, had a deep kind of hunger for a different one. And I realized that it didn't mean anything that my life wouldn't make sense to my granny; her life probably didn't make sense to *her* granny, and that made the two of us infinitely more alike than any minor difference we had about how often I prayed the rosary. Our differences, in fact, are precisely the thing that bring me closest to understanding her. I'm sure she felt different all the time.

This is the core of the connection I feel to Sinéad: it's not about technical similarities, biographies, perceptions of self—all that is subject to change, anyway. Rather, she serves as a reminder to me that some lives, even when vastly different in their particularities, have similar shapes, and that certain kinds of women have been carving their lives into inconvenient shapes for as long as anyone can remember—that our challenges and ambitions and desires may not be identical, but that they often have a symmetry, a pattern, a rhyme. The great similarity between us is not found in material details but in a larger arc of our lives, one that bends toward or against the shape we appear to be born into.

My grandmother, my mother, me; a legacy of leaving, of searching for something different than what we were promised or owed, of calling our fathers and assuring them that we're going to be fine.

Lo Siento

"All Apologies"

MYRIAM GURBA

Sinéad O'Connor deserved apologies.

She deserved one from her mother.

She deserved one from the press.

She deserved one from Frank Sinatra.

She deserved one from the music industry.

She deserved one from the papacy.

She deserved apologies from so many of us.

And yet O'Connor was often the one expected to say, "I'm sorry." Because her bravado was tempered by humility, she was able to acknowledge her offenses. She apologized to her family for insulting them during a very public dispute, emphasizing that she was "nothing but remorseful" and that it was she who had been "a total A-hole." She apologized to people of pallor after saying that she never wanted to hang out with whites again, that she found them "disgusting." She apologized to talk show host Arsenio Hall for claiming that he supplied Prince with drugs. She even apologized for enacting one of the most iconic moments in television history.

On October 3, 1992, O'Connor sang Bob Marley's "War" on *Saturday Night Live*. Without preamble, she displayed a photo of Pope John Paul II and then ripped His Holiness to shreds. Next, she uttered a succinct battle cry: "Fight the real enemy."

The Monday after O'Connor's *SNL* performance, the main topic of conversation at my small Catholic high school was the rip heard around the world. Faculty, staff, and administrators were predictably horrified by what they termed O'Connor's "blasphemy." Some said that she deserved a punishment far worse than any of the abuse she'd famously suffered during childhood. Many said she would surely go to hell. "To image Christ in mind, heart, body and soul" was our school motto, and according to several nuns, O'Connor had modeled the opposite. She was a very pretty antichrist.

If the devil could take the form of a bald Irish woman gifted with musical genius, a beguiling voice, and the balls to confront the Vatican, then I was a devil worshipper. In religion class, I often asked questions meant to make the priests in charge of my spiritual education squirm. These inquiries cast doubt on stuff like the doctrine of transubstantiation and the immaculate conception, teachings that seemed silly to me. O'Connor's *SNL* transgression put my little jabs in context; I was an amateur. By shredding an image of the pope on live television, O'Connor condemned the Church. By shredding an image of the pope on live television, O'Connor stood up for kids. It was strange and awe-inspiring to witness an adult risk her career for our sake. Usually, grown-ups were out for themselves. Usually, we were left to fend for ourselves. We were left to figure out how to care for one another.

At parties, kids whispered about who to avoid. Members of the boys' soccer team warned about Father A, a charismatic wit who often led Saturday evening mass. When Father A was suddenly dispatched to

Africa without explanation, soccer boys exchanged knowing glances. I wished my math teacher would get sent to another continent. He was a member of the laity who had married a former student, and this man would creep up behind me to massage my shoulders, caress my neck, and play with my hair. He gave me a gift once. Clothes. I never complained to the administration. How could I? The man was in charge of my grade, I wanted to pass his class, and I knew he was vindictive. I'd watched my teacher take revenge against a girl who had disobeyed him. He fetched a jump rope from a box of athletic supplies and whipped her with it. The girl cried.

During lunch period, I told the classmate who I was madly in love with that what O'Connor had done was brilliant. Isabel agreed. She'd recently adopted O'Connor as her idol, and stolen her look, shaving off her shoulder-length hair and replacing her sneakers with a pair of combat boots bought at the army surplus store. When I finally mustered the courage to confess my feelings to Isabel, she showered me with handwritten love poems and mixtapes. She covered my neck with hickeys.

I never had to buy any cassettes or CDs of O'Connor's music.

Isabel pirated them all for me.

When things ended with my first true lesbian love, I consoled myself with music. One of the songs that soothed my aching heart was Nirvana's "All Apologies." On a stage adorned with flickering black candles and white lilies, the band performed an acoustic version of the song on MTV's *Unplugged*. I used our VCR to record the performance and played it so much that the tape became fuzzy. I delighted when Cobain growled that everyone is gay. The lyrics wormed their way into my melancholy fantasies, and while their meaning remains a mystery, their impact was clear. "All Apologies" made me feel as if my wounded heart had wings. One day, they would be strong enough to take me away from a place where priests controlled my destiny and where schoolgirls broke my heart.

When was the last time you apologized?

When was the last time you meant it?

Eight months after O'Connor's *SNL* performance, *The Irish Times* published a letter by her. In it, she offered no apologies. Instead, she reminded readers of her name.

Sinéad O'Connor (the father)
Sinéad O'Connor (the son)
Sinéad O'Connor (the holy ghost)

She insisted that readers honor her humanity, a futile project.

When you're required to assert it, you've already failed.

"Stop hurting me," she begged.

Her plea went unanswered.

On December 6, 1993, Nirvana released "All Apologies" as a double A-side single.

Its companion track was "Rape Me."

Cobain told an audience that the song was about "hairy, sweaty, macho, redneck men. Who rape."

I didn't like the song.

It was too easy to misconstrue.

An early recording of "Rape Me" features the sound of an infant wailing. That baby was Frances Bean, daughter of Courtney Love and Cobain. The musicians had married in 1992, and Frances sat on her father's lap while he worked, belting out lyrics that would stir controversy.

I do not blame Frances for wailing.

On April 5, 1994, an electrician discovered Cobain in his Seattle home. At first, he thought the musician was sleeping. Then, he noticed blood trickling from the dead man's ears. A self-inflicted gunshot wound had ended his life. As usual, misogynists blamed his wife for his death. Some even accused Love of murdering him. As evidence that she had pushed him to suicide, fans pointed to "All Apologies," a song that Cobain had dedicated to Love and their daughter, a song recorded one year before Love and Cobain married.

In a photo taken at the MTV Video Music Awards in 1993, Cobain and O'Connor look vibrant. Cobain holds a cherubic Frances, and both make goofy faces. Love wears a white halter dress and holds a baby bottle less than half full. She stands between her husband and O'Connor whose smile looks genuine. Wholesome.

It's bittersweet to see her this way. Anything but bloodless.

Last year, when I learned that O'Connor had died, I wept.

I knew that wherever she was, Isabel was weeping harder.

Obituaries proliferated.

It was both gratifying and maddening to witness so many acknowledge that O'Connor had been right about so many things.

It's easy to admit that your enemy was right once she's dead.

If you want to listen to O'Connor quietly sing "All Apologies," you can. It's on her album *Universal Mother*. *SPIN* describes O'Connor's version of the song as both "bloodless" and "chillingly beautiful." I agree with the latter assessment, but I'm not sure what the critic meant by *bloodless*. By the time O'Connor recorded the album, Cobain had already ended his life, using a method that was anything but bloodless. When a reporter asked O'Connor about the photograph of her, Cobain, Love, and Frances shot at the MTV Video Music Awards, she said, "I was feeling very sorry for him, and I couldn't tell you why, but I thought, 'Oh my God, that's a man that's suffering.'"

Cobain was her mirror.

When O'Connor sings that everyone is gay, she does so with utter delicacy.

"All Apologies" had one set of mysterious meanings when Cobain and O'Connor were alive. Now that they're not, the song assumes another set of mysterious meanings.

What is the best apology you've ever given?

What is the best apology you've ever received?

How many apologies are you waiting to receive?

What are they for?

O'Connor's favorite part of the Bible was the Old Testament. She especially enjoyed scriptures involving prophets.

I hope she saw herself in them.

I hope that she counted herself among them.

The end of "All Apologies" is incantatory.

All in all is all we are to infinity.

I learned more about how to lead an ethical life from Sinéad O'Connor than I did from any priest at Catholic school.

All in all, I'm much better at offering apologies than forgiving.

O'Connor is often misrepresented as an unapologetic bitch. She was far from that. She was generous with both apologies and forgiveness.

She understood the velocity of grace.

She understood how it could move between two people.

Mother and child.

Mother and world.

Mother and universe.

To apologize in Spanish, one says, "*Lo siento.*"

That translates to, "I feel it."

Spanish is the language of my mother, and in that language, I offer our apologies to all of the prophets who went unheeded.

Lo siento.

Lo siento.

Lo siento.

Lo siento.

Lo siento.

Lo siento.

Todo es todo es todo lo que somos.

Amen.

Ghosts

"Molly Malone"

NALINI JONES

In October 2002, Sinéad O'Connor and her band played back-to-back nights at Vicar Street in Dublin, the final stop of her first Irish tour in six years. The shows marked the release of her album of traditional songs earlier that month, a project O'Connor called *Sean-Nós Nua,* meaning "old style new" in Gaelic, and the sets featured her interpretations of those old ballads alongside a few hits. One of the performances was released as a concert film the following August. By then its title—*Goodnight, Thank You, You've Been a Lovely Audience*—had a pointed new meaning, as O'Connor had announced four months earlier that she would be "retiring from the music business in order to pursue a different career." The DVD liner notes, written by Cole Moreton, acknowledged her intent in a kind of lament. After describing the power of her singing voice, from "the warrior wail" to "the whisper that is not a whisper; when she sings so quietly her voice seems about to crack but . . . the note stays pure and true," he wonders, "How can anyone who is capable of doing such a thing give it up?"

The reasons O'Connor offered—her wish for a private life, her evocation of celebrities compelled to surrender so many "pieces" of themselves that they have "nothing left of themselves to give"—seem born of deep exhaustion. By 2003, O'Connor had endured sixteen years of intense public scrutiny. She'd had little initiation in the music business when *The Lion and the Cobra* catapulted her into the spotlight. Before that, she was simply a girl writing poems and stories. A convent school nun gave her an acoustic guitar and Bob Dylan songbook, and O'Connor began ditching classes to go busking. She placed a single advertisement in a music magazine: *singer seeking band*, and within months had dropped out of school. She was eighteen when she signed her first record contract, still a teenager when she recorded vocals for a song she cowrote with The Edge. By 1990, *I Do Not Want What I Haven't Got* topped the pop charts.

The sudden stardom must have felt like a thrill ride: spectacular heights, bewildering turns, sickening plunges. Imagine a scout for a major label invites you to record demos "about a fortnight" after burying your mother. Imagine giving birth to your first child three weeks before the release of your debut. Imagine you're nominated right out of the gate for a Grammy, invited to sing at the live ceremony, suddenly navigating everything that feels right and wrong about being there. Imagine shaving your head as a message of solidarity to artists who had been excluded; and tying an infant onesie to the back of your jeans as a message to music executives who disapproved of rock star mothers. Imagine using your body in every way possible—your voice, your hair, your choice of clothes, your feet pounding the rhythm in combat boots, your arms swinging wide with no other dancers on stage, no movement but your own—not only to make your art but to insist on remaining yourself.

There is a part we don't need to imagine, if we have been twenty. Remember how it feels to be so insistent before we're entirely certain who we will turn out to be. Or as O'Connor sang in "The Emperor's

New Clothes," "How could I possibly know what I want when I was only twenty-one?"

I was almost twenty when *I Do Not Want What I Haven't Got* seemed to be playing in every dorm room. At first I listened to the full album in the order O'Connor presented the songs—a lost joy, perhaps, in this age of streaming. But before long I knew my favorites. In my reckoning, "Black Boys on Mopeds" was a brilliant contemporary protest song. I still bow down to O'Connor's nerve in beginning with "Margaret Thatcher on TV," which ought to have tanked any respectable pop song; Mrs. Thatcher is not generally considered lyric material. But O'Connor squarely placed her—and by extension the conservative government—at the center of a continuum of hypocrisy and racial injustice. At the same time, within the framing of the song, the former prime minister is reduced to a talking head while all the emotional resonance belongs to the singer and "my boy." I considered this a master stroke.

This means that at the height of her pop star success, I didn't think of Sinéad O'Connor solely as a pop star. It seemed to me she was up to something more: an artist whose songwriting ethos and vocal style tipped toward folk music. On my mixtapes, "Black Boys on Mopeds" came between Billy Bragg's "The World Turned Upside Down" and Sweet Honey in the Rock singing "Are My Hands Clean?"

But I have always seen the world through folk-colored glasses. In the sixties, my father, Robert L. Jones, tumbled from the folk clubs and coffeehouses of Cambridge, Massachusetts, into talent scouting during the early days of the Newport Folk Festival. He and Ralph Rinzler made their way across huge swathes of the country, through the bayous of Louisiana, the mining towns of Appalachia, the Georgia Sea Islands, listening to whomever might be playing in the bars or squares or dance halls, and inviting the best of them to come perform at Newport for a national audience. This launched my father's lifelong career producing music events and touring with jazz musicians for George Wein. In 1985, when George revived the Newport Folk Festival, Dad served as its producer for over twenty years. By the time I was in high school, I was on his staff.

We never liked what was mealy or pious or singsong, the lampoonable styles that most people mean when they disparage folk music. To me, folk is made of sterner stuff: the traditional forms my father championed; songs that speak truth to power; songs that reflect a keen narrative tradition; songs of laborers, migrant workers, miners, soldiers, cowboys, gamblers, girls who run off, girls who stay. I was interested in the stories and instrumental stylings that émigrés carried with them when they crossed the water to new lands, or what chain gangs sang to endure their labor. Blues, Cajun, zydeco, bluegrass, gospel, shape note singing, second line brass bands, American roots music, and the kind of country that doesn't rely on a slick twist of phrase. In the mid- to late '90s, world music began to be seriously represented on folk programs. And festival rosters were full of songwriters who were building on all these narrative traditions to craft stories of our own days: from John Prine to Keb' Mo', Conor Oberst to Gillian Welch, Lucinda Williams to the Indigo Girls.

This was how I viewed Sinéad: among those voices, with work that could take its place in that lineage. The recording industry couldn't settle on how to label her. Stores stocked her albums in pop bins, her first Grammy nomination was for rock, and her 1991 win was for Best Alternative Album. I have no particular quarrel with any of those assignations, except to note that ultimately they are marketing devices, intended to make people feel comfortable about what they buy. It's true that some artists work explicitly within those boundaries in order to thrive. But the most interesting artists, the groundbreaking artists, aren't seeking to make people comfortable. They "wade in the water," to borrow an idea from the spiritual, knowing full well that "God's gonna trouble the water," and maybe even welcoming it.

Trouble was part of O'Connor's core artistic identity; whatever the labels tried to call her, she thought of herself as punk. So it's not surprising that she waded into all sorts of waters. We all know the lines she refused to cross, the stands she decided to take. She resolved, even in song, to "live by my own policies." I never thought of her choices as political marginalia because they seemed central to her work, as though she would not have been able to sing so openly or powerfully without articulating other (to her) inescapable truths. This gave an edge to whatever she did, an appealing tension between the beauty of her voice or the delicacy of her love songs and the rebel who would not back down.

So it makes sense that she did not issue a statement about the abuses of the Catholic Church, carefully worded and vetted by publicists, the way other celebrities might make use of their platforms. She ripped a photo of the pope as the final note of a performance, her version of a smashed guitar or kicked amp. And it was not just any photo but one with personal meaning, a photo that once belonged to her mother and hung in her home. To my way of thinking, O'Connor was not simply trying to make a point; she was finding an outlet for such a tangle of rage and sorrow, both personal and communal, that it could only begin to find expression in art.

She must have expected resistance. But the waves of vitriol that came pouring over her were staggering and relentless. A person could drown in such waters. Imagine the pull of those tides, adored, despised, adored, despised. Imagine trying to keep your head up for so many years. Imagine what you do when you're so depleted that you fear you'll go under.

These were the conditions that led to Sinéad O'Connor's attempt to withdraw from public life. But first, it seems, they led to *Sean-Nós Nua*. "This is a record I've wanted to make for a very long time, and it is very much my own voice, in a way I wouldn't have been able to do with pop records," she explained in *The Song of Heart's Desire*, a documentary about the creation of the album. The conventional read might be that traditional music on a small Irish label was a step backward, but O'Connor understood her choice as essential and empowering. "I feel creatively, as a songwriter or singer, that I won't be able to move forward until I sing these songs . . . like it's all in there, just bursting to come out."

The project was also a release from the expectations of major labels, a chance to collaborate and explore. Ultimately none of the tracks are strictly *sean-nós*, a traditional Irish style of singing that is fully unaccompanied and features long melodic lines with elaborate, often melismatic, phrasing. All the songs, even those in Gaelic, have at least some light accompaniment; and the arrangements combine traditional Irish instruments with the loose, rolling rhythms of reggae, a warm sound O'Connor loved.

"I wanted somehow to drag the songs a little into the twenty-first century," she said in an interview with Irish broadcaster Pat Kenny. "Obviously they apply to this kind of century."

Perhaps the song that seems least likely to apply to this century is "Molly Malone," the old story of a fishmonger who dies of a fever. If the song feels tired, it's for good reason; it's made the rounds through generations not only in Ireland but in English-speaking communities all over the world. I first heard it from my mother, who grew up singing it in a Catholic suburb of Mumbai. It's likely her family learned it from the Irish priests who came to her neighborhood parishes. In Mum's repertoire, "Molly" belonged to a suite of songs about tragic deaths: Clementine, lost beneath the waters, or the parents in the epically mawkish "Give Me a Ticket to Heaven," in which an orphan begs a stationmaster for a train ticket to visit her departed dad. The songs all had the feel of caricature, with their cockles and mussels and melodrama. I understood them as a way my mother hoped to pass down her belief in heaven, though "Molly" also signaled her family's allegiance to Ireland. This connection seemed both truly felt and bonkers—in the peculiar way that empires forge bonkers connections—since I don't think Mum actually saw Dublin until we were grown. Her brother was named Patrick, she offered as evidence of kinship.

Later I understood that everyone laid claim to "Molly": not just the Irish or my Indian family, but any number of American artists, from Danny Kaye to Pete Seeger. The tramp in *A Clockwork Orange* sings it, in a shot that begins with his hand on a bottle and widens to show the poor old drunk alone in a tunnel, "howling away at the filthy songs of his fathers," about to be beaten to a pulp. Bing Crosby and Rosemary Clooney riffed off the original in "The Daughter of Molly Malone," a swingy, big-band number—up-tempo and campy—featuring a red-haired daughter "a-ziggin and zaggin" in a Volkswagen, still selling her wares alive, alive-oh. In Ireland, the song has become an unofficial anthem and Molly herself a landmark after a statue was commissioned to mark Dublin's first millennium in 1988. This representation seems to envision a fishmonger by day and (in a questionable association with sweetness) a prostitute by night, wearing a dress so revealing that she's been nicknamed "The Tart with the Cart" and "The Trollop with the Scallop." The tourist practice of rubbing her chest for good luck has discolored her bronze bust, prompting a local busker to launch a 2024 campaign to leave "Molly mAlone."

Molly died of fever, but clearly the song had been flogged to death by the time Sinéad O'Connor decided to give it a go. Did the world need another version?

Incredibly, yes. Her voice is the centerpiece, haunting and reverent, a nod to the project's *sean-nós* roots and to the song itself. "Molly Malone" is a ghost story, after all, and O'Connor honored the starkness of the original narrative, stripping away instrumental embellishments. And she veers away from the (strangely ubiquitous) lilting, singsong arrangements that over time turned a lament into a broadly nostalgic emblem of "Dublin's fair city."

The effect of these choices is a stunning authenticity. O'Connor slowed the tempo to the halting progress of a barrow over cobblestones. Her delivery is straightforward and somehow otherworldly, relying on the uncanny power of her voice. Even the lines that are easiest to ridicule—cockles, mussels, alive, alive-oh—seem deliberate, refreshed, lingering like the calls of real street vendors. I remembered the cries of the banana man in the neighborhood where my mother grew up, the way his voice trailed through the air like a baited line, cast far and long to see what he might catch.

Any song that has tumbled through so many generations gives rise to variants, lyrics that change a bit from singer to singer. Some versions claim the loss of Molly for the speaker: "And that's how I lost my sweet Molly Malone." That suggestion of a lover frames the whole song: the grief for Molly is chiefly individual. O'Connor sang, "She died of a fever, and no one could save her, and that was the end of sweet Molly Malone." It's a small but beautiful emphasis; Molly's loss becomes communal.

For me, that sense of the communal resonates because I see something communal in O'Connor's impulse to turn toward this material. At a time when life in the spotlight threatened to overwhelm her, she turned to the songs her father taught her when she was small, songs she had known for as long as she knew who she was. But it was not an act of retreat.

"To do these songs, I think you do have to have a certain relationship with suffering," she said in *The Song of Heart's Desire*. "The people who pull off a lot of them are people who aren't frightened of big emotion or suffering or difficult feelings . . . [They're not] afraid to be shattered by a song . . . Sometimes you can just avoid a song because it can make you cry . . . but those are the ones you should sing."

It's a reason any of us might turn to folk music, to feel grounded again in a tradition, to find our place in that lineage, to come home.

"What I love about these songs is they all have very powerful ghosts in them . . . who have something to say from centuries ago to us now," she explained to Pat Kenny during their 2002 interview. "The songs are the ones that do the talking . . . . To sing them, often you have to kind of operate almost as a medium in some ways. You move your own personality aside and you allow the ghost to come up through you."

Sean-Nós Nua is out of print. The young son O'Connor shared with one of the album's producers is gone also, a tragedy from which O'Connor could not recover. A year and a half later, she herself died. So much of what grew from this project has passed from this world.

What is with us still are her renditions of these songs. Not ghosts, after all; alive.

Truthful Witness

"Horse on the Highway"

ALLYSON McCABE

"If only I can fight off the voices of my parents and gather a sense of self-esteem. Then I'll be able to REALLY sing."

—Sinéad O'Connor, in an open letter published in the Irish Times *on June 10, 1993*

In her memoir, *Rememberings,* Sinéad said the best way to know her is through her music. Though I agree, her advice begs the question of *how* to know Sinéad through her music. Shortly after my book *Why Sinéad O'Connor Matters* was published in May 2023, I was scheduled to appear at a bookstore in conversation with *Washington Post* arts reporter Geoff Edgers. The day before the event, Geoff sent me an email with an audio file attached. Would I like to have a listen?

Back in 2020 the *Washington Post* had dispatched Geoff to California to cover Sinéad's first performances in years, a string of small concerts that doubled as a trial run for a full-scale comeback tour. Instead of flying with her band from San Francisco to Los Angeles, Sinéad caught a ride with Geoff, ostensibly so she could smoke. She soundtracked the road trip and told dirty jokes, but their conversation turned serious when she spoke about her teenage son Shane's lifelong struggle with depression and how hard it was to be so far away when he needed her.

After the trip, Geoff visited Sinéad in Ireland, where she brought up Shane again. One night she texted to ask if she could share a song she'd recorded on her front porch. The request came with a disclaimer that read, "It's a really s--- demo with a karaoke mike and a child's guitar and a Dictaphone app and a chest infection." To punctuate her self-criticism, Sinéad named the song, "Horse on the Highway Audio Rough as Shit."

When I listened to the file, the song *was* rough as shit, but not for the reasons Sinéad stated. After you hear the sound of her setting up the recording, she begins to strum a slow, sparse ballad. Then in a hoarse, anguished voice she sings about a dream of being on fire. As the flames rise, she hears a voice calling out for her. "You're too young to be addicted and running around like you have no parents," Sinéad tells the addressee, her voice worn and forlorn. She's too old to chase him, begs him to come home, and tells him that his presence is as essential to her as water. Then Sinéad closes with a bittersweet resolution: "Tonight I will dream we are in heaven/Sitting underneath that apple tree/Not being at sixes or at sevens/Just being with you being with me."

Not only did Sinéad share this heartbreaking song with Geoff—she also shared it with *The Irish Sun,* which posted it on its website. Her unguardedness may seem surprising, but Sinéad never held back from revealing her full self to anyone, even though very few of us were prepared. After she had an exchange with a reporter, she might fret about the self-exposure, alternate between admitting and denying that her music was autobiographical, then follow with an emotional email or text to retract and/or reconfirm what she just said. Most journalists misread these exchanges as signs of her mental instability, not as the fraught self-expression of an artist who needed to be heard and rarely was.

I was well aware of Sinéad's reputation as a challenging subject by the time I interviewed her for NPR's *Morning Edition* ahead of the 2021 publication of *Rememberings*. By then the pandemic had waylaid her tour plans and she'd been in a year-long treatment program for trauma and addiction. Her publicist warned me ahead of our taping that Sinéad was still fragile and advised me to avoid any questions that could be "triggering." As it turned out, Sinéad was ready to talk about everything, but I wasn't.

My assignment was to produce a brief overview of Sinéad's career and significance as an artist. As I prepared by wading through past profiles and interviews, I became outraged as I discovered how often Sinéad was right and how often others were wrong about her. I also listened to her musical catalog again, shocked to learn it was so much bigger, richer, and more diverse than I'd previously known. Journalists are conditioned to maintain distance from our subjects so we won't distort or editorialize the stories we report, but as I kept digging into my research, it became harder to remain neutral.

To manage this conflict, I doubled down on my resolve to keep our interview totally "professional." That meant it was okay for me to ask Sinéad about how she found her voice in a Catholic girls' reform school, how she refused to let her recording label control her look and sound, and how her *Saturday Night Live* appearance impacted her career. But it also meant we would not talk about life offstage. When Sinéad asked if I had kids, I immediately deflected. When she told me about her kids, I didn't ask follow-up questions. And I certainly didn't tell her that I understood what she meant when she said she was determined to be the mother she never had, even though that was an experience we shared.

There were valid reasons for me not to acknowledge that connection—after all, this was her story and not mine. Further, my editor would not have approved of the disclosure or its implications for my objectivity. But not acknowledging that I'd also become a mother after surviving an abusive childhood compromised my ability to make conscious and deliberate choices about what to share and what to hold back. It also meant that I couldn't account for what I knew to be true beyond what could be ascertained by my reporting: that from the outset of her career, her goals had nothing to do with achieving pop stardom. Nor was she an enfant terrible who broke the rules just to gain attention. Rather, Sinéad was documenting her journey of recovery through music, a healing process that had to begin with the expression of pain, anger, and sadness.

That's why Sinéad spoke unflinchingly about being abused by her mother and lashed out against that abuse in her earliest songs. That's also why she was stretched on her mother's grave, the mother who caused as much sorrow dead as she did when she was alive, the mother whose memory haunted Sinéad and provoked the tear in the video for "Nothing Compares 2 U" that made her a superstar. It's also why the first song Sinéad performed on *SNL,* "Success Has Made a Failure of Our Home"—to which she added the lyric "You're killing me, and am I not your girl?"—was one she used to sing to tame her mother's rages. It's why destroying the photo of Pope John Paul II, which had been her mother's beloved memento of his visit to Ireland, was about more than exposing the Church's complicity in perpetuating child abuse.

Over and over again Sinéad told us and showed us the real enemy was the origin story that her mother wrote for her, a story of abuse, shame, and silence. Sinéad was determined to openly confront that narrative and write her story anew, drawing connections between the suffering she endured and the injustices suffered by millions, generation after generation. After *SNL* Sinéad continued that courageous work in deeply personal songs such as "Red Football" and "Famine," in which she gave voice to Ireland's historical trauma. There can be no path forward without remembering, grieving, and forgiving, Sinéad rightly observed on an album she called *Universal Mother*. Then she followed with *Faith and Courage*, two pillars of her hard-won renewal.

By then, many people had stopped listening to Sinéad's music, having written her off as a heretic, or worse, irreparably cracked. But her willingness to keep singing and speaking out had a profound impact, including in the place where her story began, the mother country she sometimes half-jokingly called "Direland." Sinéad's impulse to throw her arms around the world and nurture it unconditionally was only part of her broader refusal to let herself be defined by her abusive childhood or to repeat it. Her decision to become a mother to four children was yet another affirmation of her desire to bring life into the world and to give it the care she had not been given.

When I read an advance copy of *Rememberings* ahead of our NPR interview, I knew from my own experience how high the stakes of motherhood must have been for her, particularly in raising her son Shane, the child she described as most like her in appearance and temperament. I knew firsthand what it's like to do your best and still feel like you're always failing, how difficult it is to fight off the internalized voice of an abusive parent telling you that you're unprepared, unworthy, and doomed to fail. I knew it and yet I held it all back, censoring us both and muting the conversation we all need to have if we want to break the cycle that protects predators and silences survivors.

When I started writing the book that grew out of that profile, I knew I would have to honor Sinéad's bravery by trying to redress my failing, which necessitated being honest with myself and my readers about my experiences and how they informed the story I was writing, this time without hiding behind the reporter's microphone. And by following Sinéad's lead and revealing myself, I hoped that I could open up the space for my readers to feel seen, too—a cathartic space of hope and possibility.

What I did not know was that as I was coming to the end of that process, Sinéad would lose Shane to suicide. I closed my book by talking about a note she posted on Twitter days after his funeral. Apologizing to fans who expressed concern for her mental health, Sinéad said she was going to the hospital. However, she also said that this was just a delay and vowed that she was going to "find Shane." I wrote that I believed her, taking that statement literally.

It was so hard for me to write that and I desperately wanted to be wrong. After a year-long absence from the public eye, Sinéad released "The Skye Boat Song," theme music for the television show *Outlander*, in February 2023. In March she accepted the RTÉ Choice Music Prize for Classic Irish Album for *I Do Not Want What I Haven't Got*. And in early July she reappeared on social media, announcing plans for a forthcoming album and tour. But then, just weeks later, Sinéad was dead.

When I heard the news, I was shattered. But when I was finally ready to listen to "Horse on the Highway" again it sounded different to me. This time the flames in the first verse still recalled the flames in the music video for "Troy" and their return in "Fire on Babylon." But in the final verse I could hear Sinéad resolving in her music what could not be resolved in life: she didn't want Shane to be alone or die alone. I came to understand this song not only as a reflection of her despair, but also the depth of her love.

Although the coroner attributed Sinéad's death to "natural causes," I think she would have likely described it in more spiritual terms, as a calling home, and I'd believe her about that, too. Today she's still very present to me in and through her music. I can hear Sinéad as the teenager who nicks a pair of gold shoes for her friend so she can wear them to a Pretenders concert, the reform-school girl who's loved by the nun who sees her rebellion as life-sustaining, the young woman who's riotous, loud, and profane, but sings like an angel.

Sinéad was the truthful witness who taught me that telling the whole truth, even the hardest truth, is the only way to heal, to make hope out of hopelessness, and to really sing. There are parts of this story that are still rough as shit, but others that are a triumph, not the least of which was Sinéad's relentless fight, her ability to transform her pain into something beautiful and enduring. "I will live by my own policies," Sinéad told us from the very start, "I will sleep with a clear conscience, I will sleep in peace."

ACKNOWLEDGMENTS

Sinéad O'Connor's unexpected death in 2023 unleashed a global outpouring of grief and affection for the singer, of which this book is one small ripple. We would like to thank everyone who responded to our call for submissions with such enthusiasm and insight; we're sad we could not include every essay pitched in this volume, but we're grateful for the wholesale support of her ever-growing, cross-generational network of fans. We are also wildly grateful to our agent, Mariah Stovall, for shepherding and polishing this project, and finding it the perfect home at One Signal. Mariah, we could not have done this without you! At One Signal, executive editor Nick Ciani and assistant editors Hannah Frankel and Abby Mohr have been wonderfully perceptive advocates and guides, and our deep thanks also go out to the rest of the One Signal team, including copy editor Lisa Nichols and publicist Maria Mann. Thank you also to Nana-Ama Danquah for some early brainstorming.

Above all, thank you to our contributors for bringing their talent and vulnerability to these pages. And, of course, thank you to Sinéad O'Connor, whose bravery, artistry, and blazing moral compass continue to inspire us all.

ENDNOTES

For Shuhada: "Heroine" by Sharbari Zohra Ahmed

1 *"whereby you will reach your target . . .":* Sahih Al-Bukhari, Volume 8, Hadith 470, https://www.islamawareness.net/Hadith/htopic_moderation.html.

Feel No Pain: "Mandinka" by Sinéad Gleeson

17 *"the oppression in my own home"*: Sinéad O'Connor, *Rememberings* (Dey Street Books, June 1, 2021), p. 204.

Listen to the Man at the Liquor Store:
"Drink Before the War" by Millicent Souris

47 *"all I could do was make music"*: *Rememberings*, p. 86.

49 *"truth of how bad it was":* IrishCentral Staff, "Sinéad O'Connor's Torment as a Victim of the Catholic Church's Magdalene Laundries," *IrishCentral Newsletters*, July 27, 2023, https://www.irishcentral.com/culture/sinead-oconnor-magdalene-laundry.

49 *September of 1996:* Another thing that happened in September 1996, just for context of time . . . Tupac Shakur was shot and killed.

49 *"I was scared there":* IrishCentral Staff, "Sinéad O'Connor's Torment as a Victim of the Catholic Church's Magdalene Laundries," *IrishCentral Newsletters*, July 27, 2023, https://www.irishcentral.com/culture/sinead-oconnor-magdalene-laundry.

Girl You Better Try to Have Fun:
"Nothing Compares 2 U" by Megan Stielstra

92 *"world and placed above it":* Letter Sinéad O'Connor wrote to the Academy, per the *Los Angeles Times* in February 1991. Robert Hilburn, "O'Connor Pulls Out of Grammys: Irish Singer Attacks the Music Industry for 'False, Materialistic Values,'" *Los Angeles Times*, February 2, 1991, https://www.latimes.com/archives/la-xpm-1991-02-02-ca-227-story.html.

As You Summon Steel:
"The Last Day of Our Acquaintance" by Sonya Huber

105 *"when I nod my head," he writes:* Jason Tibbetts, "The Last Day of Our Acquaintance," *Thank You for Hearing Me: The Definitive Sinéad O'Connor Discography,* https://www.thankyouforhearingme.com/songs/last_day_of_our_acquaintance.html.

105 *"a business arrangement and a love affair":* Mikal Gilmore, "I Do Not Want What I Haven't Got," *Rolling Stone*, January 22, 1997, https://www.rollingstone.com/music/music-album-reviews/i-do-not-want-what-i-havent-got-94290/.

105 *with a court battle lasting until 2019*: Rob Tannenbaum, "Sinéad O'Connor's radical honesty," *Washington Post*, July 27, 2023; https://www.washingtonpost.com/arts-entertainment/2023/07/27/sinead-oconnor-mtv-fearless-uncompromising.

"Sinead O'Connor Explains Cancelled Tour in Open Letter," *Rolling Stone*, May 9, 2012. https://www.rollingstone.com/music/music-news/sinead-oconnor-explains-canceled-tour-in-open-letter-205226/; Aodhan O'Faolain, "Sinead O'Connor reaches 'amicable' court settlement with former manager," *Irish Times*, May 1, 2019, https://www.irishtimes.com/news/crime-and-law/courts/high-court/sinead-o-connor-reaches-amicable-court-settlement-with-former-manager-1.3877330.

106 *toured with her in 2013:* Eddie Rowley, "How Sinéad O'Connor's Love for First Husband John Reynolds Lasted a Lifetime," *Sunday World*, July 29, 2023, https://www.sundayworld.com/showbiz/music/how-sinead-oconnors-love-for-first-husband-john-reynolds-lasted-a-lifetime-a722920883.html.

106 *to bring her home to Ireland.* Geoff Edgers, "Sinead O'Connor is still in one piece," Washington *Post*, March 18, 2020, https://www.washingtonpost.com/lifestyle/style/sinead-oconnor-is-still-in-one-piece/2020/03/18/301a4230-621d-11ea-acca-80c22bbee96f_story.html.

You Are Something: "Don't Cry for Me Argentina" by Mieke Eerkens

119 *"special meaning for you, I think?": Tros* interview, https://youtu.be/jIf_JQM7GM4?si=xuLKao2PyfPgORWX.

120 *an interview in 2017: Dr. Phil Show*, September 12, 2017, https://youtu.be/_H1DsWsKLE8?si=wdxPuiTLkVRCzhQg, https://youtu.be/ktw8DSU5g30?si=ZZ1_ephMn_P_3SVu.

133 *"are worth losing your career for": Rememberings*, p. 193.

St. Sinéad: "Famine" by Lauretta Hannon

147 *"I would wish for everyone":* Paula D'Arcy, *Stars at Night: When Darkness Unfolds as Light* (Cincinnati, OH, Franciscan Media, 2016), book publicity material.

147 *"are worth being a pariah for": Rememberings*, p. 266.

148 *"with the music business": Rememberings*, p. 177.

150 *"and that was sing": Rememberings*, p. 276.

Sunshower: "The Wolf Is Getting Married" by Martha Bayne

155 *from a conversation with a London cabbie:* Oliver Good, "Sinead O'Connor Mounts a Triumphant Return," *The National*, February 20, 2012, https://thenational-the-national-staging.web.arc-cdn.net/arts-culture/music/sinead-o-connor-mounts-a-triumphant-return-1.404089.

Precious to Me: "My Special Child" by Jill Christman

168 *"That's what punks do": The Blindboy Podcast*, May 26, 2021.

170 *"chosen" these parents:* Bob Guccione Jr., "Sinéad O'Connor: SPIN's 1991 Cover Story, 'Special Child,'" *Spin*, September 18, 2015, https://www.spin.com/2015/09/sinead-oconnor-interview-spin-30-cover-story/.

170 *"solution to an Irish problem":* "Sinéad O'Connor Joins Abortion-Rights Rally in Dublin in 1992." NowThis Impact, YouTube, https://www.youtube.com/watch?v=_1uAne8AQLo.

171 *"like a little planet":* Sinéad O'Connor, *Rememberings* (Dey Street Books, June 1, 2021), p. 117.

171 *"The whole issue is pro-choice":* Bob Guccione Jr., "Sinéad O'Connor: SPIN's 1991 Cover Story, 'Special Child,'" *Spin*, September 18, 2015, https://www.spin.com/2015/09/sinead-oconnor-interview-spin-30-cover-story/.

Sorry for Disappointing: "Daddy I'm Fine" by Rayne Fisher-Quann

177 *with men in general:* She famously came out as a lesbian in this interview, then later clarified that it was an "overcompensation." Diane Anderson-Minshall, "Curve's 20th Anniversary Retrospective: Sinéad O'Connor," *Curve*, February 1, 2010, https://www.curvemag.com/blog/interviews/curves-20th-anniversary-retrospective-sinad-oconnor/.

177 *wanting at the time:* Diane Anderson-Minshall, "Curve's 20th Anniversary Retrospective: Sinéad O'Connor," *Curve*, February 1, 2010, https://www.curvemag.com/blog/interviews/curves-20th-anniversary-retrospective-sinad-oconnor/.

Lo Siento: "All Apologies" by Myriam Gurba

181 *"a total A-hole":* Aidan Lonergan, "Sinéad O'Connor Apologises to Her Family for Putting Them Through It Over the Years," *Irish Post*, May 16, 2017, https://www.irishpost.com/life-style/sinead-oconnor-apologises-family-putting-years-122272.

181 *found them "disgusting":* Jacob Stolworthy, "Sinéad O'Connor Apologises for Saying She 'Never Wants to Spend Time with White People Again,'" *Independent*, September 9, 2019, https://www.independent.co.uk/arts-entertainment/music/news/sinead-o-connor-white-people-twitter-rant-islam-davitt-late-show-ireland-a9097106.html.

184 *"men. Who rape":* https://www.youtube.com/watch?v=QKhqqB4taSE.

Ghosts: "Molly Malone" by Nalini Jones

194 *Irish broadcaster Pat Kenny:* "Sinead O'Connor Interview," Ireland 2002. YouTube, https://www.youtube.com/watch?v=lYg-1NAq8GE.

195 *leave "Molly mAlone":* James Crisp, "Stop Groping the Breasts on Molly Malone Statue, Dublin Tourists Told," *The Telegraph*, March 1, 2024, https://www.telegraph.co.uk/world-news/2024/03/01/stop-groping-breasts-on-dublins-molly-malone-campaign/.

INDEX

ABOUT THE AUTHORS

Sharbari Zohra Ahmed is an award-winning writer of film and fiction. She was on the writing team for the ABC TV Series *Quantico* and adapted the middle grade novel *Rickshaw Girl*, by Mitali Bose Perkins, into a feature film. She is the author of a novel, *Dust Under Her Feet* (Westland, 2019), and two short story collections, *The Ocean of Mrs. Nagai: Stories* (DS Books, 2013), and *The Strangest of Fruit*, forthcoming from Cheek Press in 2025.

Martha Bayne is the editor of three collections of writing about Chicago and the Midwest, most recently *The Chicago Neighborhood Guidebook* (Belt Publishing, 2019), which was named one of the best twenty-first century books about the city by *Chicago* magazine. A journalist, editor, and essayist, her work has appeared in local and national outlets, including the *Chicago Reader*, the *Chicago Reporter*, the *Baffler, Eater, Belt Magazine, PRI/The World, South Side Weekly*, and *The Rumpus*, where she was for two years the Sunday essays coeditor. A member of Theater Oobleck's artistic ensemble, she has also written work for solo performance. She currently works as the regional trade editor at the University of Illinois Press and writes a newsletter called "Range of Motion."

Stacey Lynn Brown is a poet, playwright, and nonfiction writer originally from Atlanta, Georgia. She is the author of two books of poetry, *Cradle Song* and *The Shallows*, and is the coeditor, with Oliver de la Paz, of *A Face to Meet the Faces: An Anthology of Contemporary Persona Poetry*. Her poems and essays have appeared in venues such as *Crab Orchard Review, Copper Nickel, The Rumpus,* and *Prairie Schooner*. She teaches in the MFA program at Indiana University and is currently at work on a musical and a memoir.

Neko Case is a singer, songwriter, music producer, visual artist, and writer who has built a career with her distinctive style and musical versatility. She is the author of the acclaimed memoir *The Harder I Fight the More I Love You*. In addition to her numerous critically acclaimed and Grammy-nominated solo records, Case is a founding member of The New Pornographers. She authors the newsletter "Entering The Lung" and is currently composing the musical theater adaptation of an Academy Award–winning motion picture.

May-lee Chai is the award-winning author of eleven books of fiction, nonfiction, and translation, including her latest short story collection, *Tomorrow in Shanghai,* which was a *New York Times* Editors' Choice and longlisted for The Story Prize. Her previous collection, *Useful Phrases for Immigrants,* won an American Book Award. Her writing has been awarded a National Endowment for the Arts fellowship, Asian/Pacific American Award for Literature, Gulf Coast Prize in Nonfiction, named a Kiriyama Prize Notable Book, and a recipient of an honorable mention for the Gustavus Myers Center for the Study of Bigotry and Human Rights Book Awards. Her short prose has appeared widely, including in *New England Review, New York Times Book Review, Los Angeles Times, Best Small Fictions* anthology, and has been cited as Notable in two editions of the *Best American Essays* anthology. She is a professor of creative writing at San Francisco State University and an elected member of the board of directors of the NBCC. Visit her website at may-leechai.com.

Brooke Champagne is the award-winning author of *Nola Face: A Latina's Life in the Big Easy*, published with the Crux Series in Literary Nonfiction at the University of Georgia Press. *Nola Face* was a medalist in Southern Nonfiction at the 2024 IPPY Awards, and was selected as a Best Book of 2024 by Kirkus Reviews. Her work has been selected as Notable in several editions of the *Best American Essays* anthology series, and she is Assistant Professor of Creative Writing in the MFA Program at the University of Alabama.

Jill Christman is the author of *If This Were Fiction: A Love Story in Essays* (2023 Foreword INDIES Silver Winner) and two memoirs, *Darkroom: A Family Exposure* (winner of AWP Prize for CNF) and *Borrowed Babies: Apprenticing for Motherhood*. Her essays have appeared in many anthologies and in magazines such as *Brevity, Creative Nonfiction, Fourth Genre, Iron Horse Literary Review, Longreads, The Rumpus,* and *O, The Oprah Magazine*. A 2020 NEA Literature Fellow, she teaches at Ball State University where she is a senior editor of *River Teeth: A Journal of Nonfiction Narrative* and *Beautiful Things*. Visit her at jillchristman.com.

Heidi Czerwiec is the author of the lyric essay collection *Fluid States*, selected by Dinty W. Moore as winner of Pleiades Press's 2018 Robert C. Jones Prize for Short Prose, *Crafting the Lyric Essay: Strike a Chord*, and the poetry collection *Conjoining*, and is the coeditor of *The Rose Metal Press Field Guide to Writing the Lyric Essay* and editor of *North Dakota Is Everywhere: An Anthology of Contemporary North Dakota Poets*. She writes and teaches in Minneapolis, where she is an editor for *Assay: A Journal of Nonfiction Studies*. Visit her at heidiczerwiec.com.

Mieke Eerkens is a Dutch-American writer who grew up in Los Angeles. She earned a BA in Creative Writing from San Francisco State University, an MA in English from the University of Leiden in The Netherlands, and an MFA from the University of Iowa. She has taught in the Magid Center Undergraduate Writing Program at the University of Iowa, Iowa Summer Writing Festival, UCLA Extension's Writers' Program in Los Angeles, and at Amsterdam University College and Leiden University College in The Netherlands, among others. Her writing has appeared in outlets such as *The Atlantic, The Rumpus, Los Angeles Review of Books, Catapult, Pen America, Pank, Guernica,* and *Creative Nonfiction*. Her work has further been anthologized in *Best Travel Writing 2011;* Norton's *Fakes: An Anthology of Pseudo-Interviews, Faux-Lectures, Quasi-Letters, "Found" Texts, and Other Fraudulent Artifacts*; *Water's Edge: Open to Interpretation*; and *A Book of Uncommon Prayer*. *All Ships Follow Me* (Picador, 2019), a book about her parents' respective experiences in WWII and the inheritance of war trauma, was published in 2019. She is currently working on a memoir about her younger years traveling with the circus. She lives in Amsterdam.

Rayne Fisher-Quann was born in 2001 on the hottest day of the year. She is a Brooklyn-based writer and artist best known for her blog, "internet princess." It has 65,000+ regular readers, and her essays have been read over 1 million times. Rayne's work deals with womanhood, mental illness, commodification, morality, and the formation and construction of identity in the internet age. Her first book, *Complex Female Character*, is forthcoming from Knopf.

Gina Frangello's fifth book, the memoir *Blow Your House Down: A Story of Family, Feminism, and Treason* (Counterpoint, 2021), has been selected as a *New York Times* Editors' Choice, received starred reviews in *Publishers Weekly*, *Library Journal*, and *BookPage*, and has been included on numerous "Best of 2021" lists, including at *Lit Hub*, *BookPage*, and *The Chicago Review of Books*. Her sixth book, on Elena Ferrante's Neapolitan Quartet, was released as part of IG Publishing's "Bookmarked" series in July 2024. Gina is also the author of four books of fiction, including *A Life in Men* and *Every Kind of Wanting*, which was included on several "Best of 2016" lists, including at *Chicago Magazine* and *The Chicago Review of Books*. Her first two books, *My Sister's Continent* and *Slut Lullabies*, out of print for some time, are soon being reissued by Northwestern University Press. Now a lead editor at Row House Publishing, Gina also brings more than two decades of experience as an editor, having founded both the independent press Other Voices Books and the fiction section of the popular online literary community The Nervous Breakdown. She has also served as the Sunday editor for *The Rumpus*, the faculty editor for both *TriQuarterly Online* and *The Coachella Review*, and the creative nonfiction editor for the *Los Angeles Review of Books*. Gina obtained her PhD in English/Creative Writing from the University of Illinois Chicago, with a specialization in Gender Theory. She is on the low residency MFA faculty at the University of Nevada-Reno/Tahoe and runs Circe Consulting, a full-service company for writers, with the writer Emily Rapp Black.

Madhushree Ghosh is author of the award-winning debut food narrative memoir, *KHABAAR: An Immigrant Journey of Food, Memory,* *and Family* (University of Iowa Press, 2022). As a 2023 TEDx San Diego Seeds of Change speaker highlighting food, immigration, social justice, and community, she highlighted East African refugee farming women in San Diego in her talk titled, *What We Talk About When We Talk About Food*. Her work has appeared in *Best American Essays in Food Writing* (2023), been Pushcart-nominated, and was awarded the Independent Publishers Book Awards (IPPY) Gold in the memoir/family legacy/travel category, and published in the *New York Times, Los Angeles Times,* the *Washington Post, Vogue India, Longreads, Catapult, BOMB, The Rumpus, Writer's Digest, Los Angeles Review of Books, Guernica,* and others. She runs the curated global literary salon and supper club, *KhabaarCo,* which highlights food cultures, writing, responsible travel, and mindful activism through conversations with historians, authors, chefs, and leaders.

As the daughter of refugees, an Indian immigrant to America, and a woman of color in science and in narrative nonfiction, Madhushree is an invited speaker to global food and literary festivals, universities, biotech and pharma conferences focusing on food as a social justice tool, intimate partner violence, gender pay parity, and conversations on women of color in science. San Diego–based Madhushree works in oncology diagnostics and is currently working on a second narrative memoir on the Sikh immigration to California. She teaches narrative nonfiction at Grubstreet and can be reached on social media at @writemadhushree or her website.

Sinéad Gleeson's essay collection *Constellations: Reflections from Life* won Non-Fiction Book of the Year at the Irish Book Awards and the Dalkey Literary Award for Emerging Writer. It short-listed for the Rathbones Folio Prize, the James Tait Black Memorial Prize, and the Michel Déon Prize, and has been translated into several languages.

She is the editor of four anthologies, including *The Art of the Glimpse* and the award-winning *The Long Gaze Back: An Anthology of Irish Women Writers,* and *The Glass Shore: Short Stories*. Sinéad has engaged in multi-disciplinary collaborations with artists and musicians, including commissions from The Wellcome Collection, the RHA Gallery, BBC, Rua Red Gallery, and Frieze. She is coeditor with Kim Gordon of *This Woman's Work: Essays on Music*. Her debut novel, *Hagstone,* was published in April 2024 by 4th Estate.

Stephanie Elizondo Griest is a globe-trotting author from the Texas-Mexico borderlands. Her six books include: *Around the Bloc, Mexican Enough, All the Agents and Saints,* and the forthcoming *Art Above Everything*. Widely anthologized, she has also written for the *New York Times,* the *Washington Post, The Believer, BBC,* and *Oxford American*. Her work has won a Margolis Award for Social Justice Reporting and has been supported by the Henry Luce Foundation and Lannan Foundation. Currently Professor of Creative Nonfiction at the University of North Carolina-Chapel Hill, she has performed as a Moth storyteller as well as a literary ambassador for the U.S. State Department. In 2024, she founded Testimonios Fronterizos, an endowed grant for student journalists from the border. Visit her website at www.StephanieElizondoGriest.com.

Myriam Gurba is a writer and activist. Her first book, the short story collection *Dahlia Season,* won the Edmund White Award for debut fiction. *O, The Oprah Magazine,* ranked her true crime memoir, *Mean,* as one of the best LGBTQ books of all time. *Creep,* her most recent book, was a finalist for a National Book Critics' Circle award in criticism. The *New York Times, Los Angeles Times, Harper's Bazaar, Vox,* and *Paris Review* have published her work. She is a cofounder of Dignidad Literaria, a grassroots organization committed to combatting racism in the book world. She is active in the anti-rape movement.

Lauretta Hannon is the author of *The Cracker Queen—A Memoir of a Jagged, Joyful Life* (Gotham Books, Penguin) and has been a commentator on National Public Radio's *All Things Considered,* where her stories have reached 25 million listeners. Her memoir was named "One of the Top 25 Books All Georgians Should Read" by the Georgia Center for the Book. A documentary about her story, *Raised in the South of Normal,* captured awards at film festivals across the country. *Southern Living Magazine* has named her the "Funniest Woman in Georgia."

Supporting and guiding other writers is an integral part of her mission, and her work with incarcerated women and youth has been especially meaningful.

Lauretta blogs and podcasts at laurettahannon.com and has given a TEDx Talk titled *This Sentence Will Transform Your Life*. She writes in a shed that was once the site of a storied moonshining operation.

Sonya Huber was a 2024 finalist for the PEN/Diamondstein-Spielvogel Award for the Art of the Essay and is the author of eight books, including the essay collection *Love and Industry: A Midwestern Workbook* and the craft book *Voice First: A Writer's Manifesto,* which *Publishers Weekly* called a "spirited look at craft." Her essay collection *Pain Woman Takes Your Keys and Other Essays from a Nervous System* received the Independent Publishers' Association Gold Medal for General Excellence, and has been called "important, luminous, and necessary." Her three other books of creative nonfiction include *Supremely Tiny Acts: A Memoir in a Day,* a stream-of-consciousness account of a climate action, organized by Extinction Rebellion; *Opa Nobody,* shortlisted for the Saroyan Prize; and *Cover Me: A Health Insurance Memoir*. Her work has appeared in the *New York*

Times, Creative Nonfiction, Brevity, the *Washington Post, The Atlantic, Fourth Genre,* and other outlets. She's received the 2012 Creative Nonfiction Award from *Terrain;* her essays have been named notable in multiple volumes of Best American Essays, and she teaches at Fairfield University.

Nalini Jones is the author of a story collection, *What You Call Winter,* and a forthcoming novel, *The Unbroken Coast* (Knopf, 2025). Her work has appeared in *Ploughshares, One Story,* and *Guernica,* among others, and she has been awarded an O. Henry Prize, a Pushcart Prize, and a literature fellowship from the National Endowment of the Arts. She currently teaches writing at Fairfield University; past appointments have been at Columbia University, Williams College, Yale University, and the Arcadia Center for Hellenic, Mediterranean, and Balkan Studies in Greece. A longtime producer of live music events, she continues to work at the New Orleans Jazz & Heritage Festival and Saratoga Jazz Festival.

Porochista Khakpour was born in Tehran and raised in Los Angeles's San Gabriel Valley. Her debut novel *Sons and Other Flammable Objects* (Grove, 2007) was a *New York Times* Editors' Choice, one of the *Chicago Tribune*'s Fall's Best, and the 2007 California Book Award winner in the "First Fiction" category. Her second novel *The Last Illusion* (Bloomsbury, 2014) was a 2014 "Best Book of the Year" according to NPR, *Kirkus,* Buzzfeed, Popmatters, Electric Literature, and many more. Her widely acclaimed third book, *Sick: A Memoir* (Harper Perennial, 2018) was a Best Book of 2018 according to *Time Magazine, Real Simple, Entropy, Mental Floss, Bitch Media, Autostraddle, The Paris Review, Lit Hub,* and more. It is currently in its fifth printing. Her most recent book, the essay collection *Brown Album: Essays on Exile and Identity* (Vintage, May 2020), has been praised in the *New York Times, O, The Oprah Magazine, TIME, goop, USA Today,* and many more. Her most recent book, *Tehrangeles: A Novel* (Pantheon), came out in June 2024, and was an Indie Next Pick, an NPR Book of the Day, one of *TIME*'s 25 Most Anticipated Books of 2024, as well as one of the "Best Books of 2024 (So Far)" by *Vogue, Harper's Bazaar, W*, and more. Among her many fellowships is a National Endowment for the Arts award. Her other writing has appeared in many sections of the *New York Times*, the *Los Angeles Times*, the *Washington Post*, the *Wall Street Journal, Bookforum, Elle, Slate, BOMB*, and many others. She has enjoyed residencies and fellowships at Northwestern's Academy for Alternative Journalism, MacDowell, Civitella Ranieri, Yaddo, Ucross, VCCA, Vermont Studio Center, Atlantic Center for the Arts, and more. She has taught creative writing and literature at Columbia University, Johns Hopkins University, Bucknell University, Bard College, Wesleyan University, Sarah Lawrence College, Fordham University, the University of Leipzig, and more for the past twenty years. She is a contributing editor at *Evergreen Review* and lives in NYC. For more info: www.porochistakhakpour.com.

Leah Lakshmi Piepzna-Samarasinha (she/they) is a nonbinary femme disabled writer and disability and transformative justice movement worker of Burgher and Tamil Sri Lankan, Irish and Galician/Roma ascent. They are the author or coeditor of ten books, including *The Future Is Disabled: Prophecies, Love Notes and Mourning Songs*; *Beyond Survival: Stories and Strategies from the Transformative Justice Movement* (coedited with Ejeris Dixon); *Tonguebreaker*; and *Care Work: Dreaming Disability Justice*. A Lambda Award winner, five-time Publishing Triangle finalist, winner of the 2022 Jeanne Córdova Award for a "lifetime of work documenting the complexities of disabled, queer of color, and femme experience," they are a 2020–2021 Disability Futures Fellow and longtime disabled BIPOC space maker, and are currently building Living Altars, a cultural homespace by and for QTBIPOC disabled writers and cultural workers. They are an older cousin on the stoop, a couch and porch witch, and an almost-illder.

Allyson McCabe is the author of *Why Sinéad O'Connor Matters* (University of Texas Press, 2023), which won the ASCAP Foundation Deems Taylor/Virgil Thomson Award. As a music journalist, Allyson's work is often broadcast nationally on NPR, and her byline appears in publications, including the *New York Times*, BBC Culture, *Vulture*, and *Wired*, as well as anthologies such as *Overlooked: A Celebration of Remarkable, Underappreciated People Who Broke the Rules and Changed the World*, and *Pen & Ink: Tattoos and the Stories Behind Them*. For more, please visit https://www.allysonmccabe.com.

Millicent Souris is a writer and cook living in New York. Her newsletter, "Attitude Adjustment Facility," is published bimonthly, focusing on food, culture, work, grief, and the powers that be. Previous work can be found in *Bon Appétit, The Rumpus, Heated,* and *Diner Journal,* where she was an editor-at-large. She published *How to Build a Better Pie: Sweet and Savory Recipes for Flaky Crusts, Toppers, and the Things in Between* (Quarry Books) in 2012. Sometimes she works on TV shows.

Megan Stielstra is the author of three collections: *Everyone Remain Calm, Once I Was Cool,* and *The Wrong Way to Save Your Life*. Her work appears in *Best American Essays,* the *New York Times, Chicago Tribune, The Believer, Poets & Writers, Tin House,* and elsewhere. A longtime company member with 2nd Story, she has told stories for National Public Radio, the Museum of Contemporary Art, and theaters, festivals, and classrooms across the country. She teaches creative nonfiction at Northwestern University and is the Senior Editor of Regional Titles at Northwestern University Press.

Sarah Viren is the author of two books: the essay collection *Mine,* which won the *River Teeth* Book Award and the Great Lakes College Association New Writers Award, and *To Name the Bigger Lie: A Memoir in Two Stories,* a *New York Times* Editors' Choice, a Lambda Literary Award finalist, and an NPR and *Lit Hub* best book of the year. A contributing writer for the *New York Times Magazine* and a former National Endowment for the Arts fellow, Viren teaches in the creative writing program at Arizona State University.

Lidia Yuknavitch is the author of the bestselling novels *Thrust, The Book of Joan, The Small Backs of Children,* and *Dora: A Headcase,* and the memoir *The Chronology of Water.* Her book *The Misfit's Manifesto* spawned a TED Talk, "On the Beauty of Being a Misfit," now with over 4 million views. *The Chronology of Water* is currently being adapted for film by Kristen Stewart. She lives in a Sitka and Alder forest near the Pacific Ocean with Andy and Miles Mingo. She is a very good swimmer. Her next nonfiction book lands in 2024.

Zoe Zolbrod is the author of the memoir *The Telling,* the novel *Currency,* and the novel *Coin of the Realm,* which is forthcoming from Northwestern University Press. Her essays have appeared in places such as *Salon, HuffPo,* the *Guardian,* and *The Rumpus,* where she served as the Sunday coeditor.